**More**

# Christmas
## Wrapped up!

© Scripture Union 2007
First published 2007
ISBN 978 1 84427 261 7

Scripture Union, 207–209 Queensway, Bletchley, Milton Keynes, MK2 2EB, England
Email: info@scriptureunion.org.uk
Website: www.scriptureunion.org.uk

Scripture Union Australia
Locked Bag 2, Central Coast Business Centre, NSW 2252
Website: www.scriptureunion.org.au

Scripture Union USA
P.O. Box 987, Valley Forge, PA 19482
Website: www.scriptureunion.org

Scripture quotations are from the Contemporary English Version published by HarperCollinsPublishers © 1991, 1992, 1995, American Bible Society.

British Library Cataloguing-in-Publication Data
A catalogue record of this book is available from the British Library.

Printed and bound by Henry Ling Ltd
Cover design: Paul Airy
Compiler: Christine Wright
Editorial team: Alex Taylor, Helen Gale, Alicia Wallace, Karen Evans
Artists: Pauline Adams, Lynne Breeze, Anna Carpenter, Clive Edwards, Helen Gale, Andy Gray, Eira Reeves

Scripture Union is an international Christian charity working with churches in more than 130 countries, providing resources to bring the good news about Jesus Christ to children, young people and families and to encourage them to develop spiritually through the Bible and prayer.
As well as our network of volunteers, staff and associates who run holidays, church-based events and school Christian groups, we produce a wide range of publications and support those who use our resources through training programmes.

We extend grateful thanks to all the writers and artists who regularly contribute to *Light*. Without their hard work and creativity this book could not have been produced. And thanks to our Scripture Union field and schools workers who have been willing to share their expertise and bright ideas. Every effort has been made to attribute the items correctly, but we apologise to any author or artist whose work has not been credited. Please inform the publisher and we will endeavour to put matters right in any future editions of *More Christmas Wrapped Up!*

# Contents

## Introduction

## Short talks for evangelism

## Events and parties

## Short talks for all ages

## Assembly material

## All-age services

## Family activities

## Short dramas

## Dramatised readings

Contents

# Introduction

Christmas (love it or hate it) provides both a challenge and an opportunity for churches, and *More Christmas Wrapped Up!* is full of material to help you make the most of the season!

This compilation of ideas is for you, if you've ever thought, 'Christmas again! It only seems like a couple of months since the last one. What on earth can we do this year?' If you need inspiration for short talks for any occasion, there's plenty here. You may be looking for new material for services for all ages or Christmas events, or you may simply need prayers, songs, games or stories to use with children and young people. In addition there are recipes for Christmas goodies, craft projects for all abilities and much more.

You may, on the other hand, be excited by the opportunities that Christmas brings, to present the good news to people with whom you would not normally have much contact. As you turn the pages of this book, you'll discover tried and tested ways of presenting the gospel in interesting and absorbing ways. You could try out some of the drama to increase familiarity with the story of Christmas, at the same time bringing out the meaning of the story in a new, appealing way. You could challenge families to try out the 'Family activities' at home or use the 'Dramatised readings' to bring a new focus to the words of the Bible.

Christmas is much more than a time for feasting, indulgence and overspending. I hope that this compilation of material will help you inspire people to think more deeply about what Christmas really means – God's love revealed to all people in the person of his Son, Jesus.

## Christine Wright

## Labelling Jesus

*A talk which challenges popular views about who Jesus is*

**You will need:** *A4 sheets of paper, a flip chart or whiteboard, marker pens, Blu-tack*

Before the service use the sheets of paper and marker pens to prepare examples of some of the labels that have been associated with Jesus. Examples should include the following, as well as any others that you wish to add: 'Son of Man'; 'Great teacher'; 'Magician'; 'Son of God'; 'A good man'; 'Healer'; 'Someone who cared'; 'Invention of the Gospel writers'.

Hide the labels around the meeting room. Draw three columns on the flip chart or whiteboard and head them 'Label', 'True' and 'False' respectively.

Introduce the activity by remarking that different people have had different opinions about Jesus over the years. Explain that some of those opinions are hidden around the meeting room. Invite people to hunt for the hidden labels, and return to their seats, with any that they find. When all the labels have been found, ask for them to be brought to the front one at a time and glued in the first column on the flip chart or whiteboard. As each label is placed on the board, ask the congregation to vote on whether the statement is true or false, and put a tick in the appropriate column. Be sure to fully involve the children and young people in the voting and discussion activity.

Be prepared for some disagreement on statements like 'A good man' and be prepared to comment. Sum up by saying that some of the statements are obviously out of line with what the Bible teaches and that some others are true but don't go far enough. (For example: 'great teacher' and 'good man'.) You may also need to add when the 'Invention of Gospel writers' label goes up, that there is good evidence outside the Bible for the existence of Jesus, and that it is hardly likely that the early Christians would have given up their lives for something they knew to be a lie.

Finish by drawing their attention to the label, 'Son of God'. Read Luke 1:26–33 and comment how it was an angel from heaven who told Mary that her child would be the Son of God. She found it hard to understand but was willing to trust God. This Christmas, God invites each of us to believe that Mary's child is his Son, trusting that nothing is impossible for him.

## Gifts

*A talk suitable for Christmas Day*

**You will need:** *four large gift tags with the following words written on them, and each attached to a chocolate Christmas tree decoration – gift tag 1: 'A gift ... from God'; gift tag 2: 'A gift ... for all of us'; gift tag 3: 'A gift ... of new life'; gift tag 4: 'A gift ... through Jesus'*

Hang the decorations on a Christmas tree. Many churches like to include a short time on Christmas Day when the people are encouraged to show one of their Christmas gifts. This would be a suitable time to do this.

Make the point that the best Christmas gift of all didn't come in a box or Christmas stocking.

Proceed with the talk by asking each question below in turn. *(Each time take the appropriate gift tag from the Christmas tree and offer it to a member of the congregation, inviting them to read out what it says and then allowing them to keep the small chocolate gift to eat later.)*

Who is it from? *(Give gift tag 1 to someone.)*

Read Romans 5:15 and explain briefly what 'grace' means. It means something given out of kindness, not because we deserve it. God himself has sent this gift because of his great kindness.

Who is it for? *(Give out gift tag 2.)*

Read Romans 5:15 again. Explain that God's gift was not just for a few special people, or for the people who were living when Jesus came as a baby, but it is for everyone.

What is it? *(Give out gift tag 3.)*

Read Romans 5:18. Explain that ever since the time of Adam, the first man in the Bible, people have done wrong things that did not please God. This is sin. Sin creates a barrier between God and us, but instead of punishing us for our sin, God's gift is that he sent Jesus to take the punishment for us so that we could be forgiven. Then God can accept us and offer us a new life.

How do we get it? *(Give out gift tag 4.)*

Read Romans 5:19. Jesus has been punished in our place and we can receive God's gift through accepting what Jesus has done for us.

7

## Four different hats

*A talk based on Luke 2:22–38*

**You will need:** *four different hats*

Around 700 years before Simeon and Anna were born, God had promised a messiah – someone who would save God's people. Did God's people believe it? *(Wear different hats as you illustrate what people in Simeon's day might have thought.)*

**Hat 1:** 'Yeah, well, those prophets back then were in "cloud cuckoo-land". I don't believe it.'
**Hat 2:** 'That promise was centuries ago! People believed different things then. And anyway, if it hasn't happened by now, it never will.'
**Hat 3:** 'It's a lovely thought… someone to save us; I wish it would happen, but it's probably just wishful thinking.'

People wear the same hats today when they think about the Christmas message of God sending Jesus to be our Saviour. For example:

**Hat 1:** 'The Christmas Story – it's just a story! I don't believe it really happened!'
**Hat 2:** 'Jesus lived over 2,000 years ago! We live in an age of science now – we don't need God. And anyway didn't Jesus say he would come back and he hasn't?!'
**Hat 3:** 'I love the Christmas story – you know – peace and joy. I wish it were real!'

Simeon and Anna who saw Jesus as a small baby, wore a different hat!

**Hat 4:** 'God has promised. He always keeps his promises. I trust him.'

Simeon and Anna believed what God said. Their lives showed that they believed him. It was tough waiting but they kept on trusting God. Simeon and Anna were right to trust God. Simeon saw and held Jesus. He had living proof that:

• God had kept his promise (Luke 2:29).
• God had sent a saviour for all people (Luke 2:30,32).

Which hat are we wearing? Are we ready to take the Christmas story seriously and believe what God has said?

Those of us who are already wearing 'hat 4' should follow Simeon and Anna's example:

• Thank and praise God (Luke 2:28–32,38).
• Tell others about Jesus (Luke 2:38).

## Christmas surprises!

*A talk using simple pictures drawn onto OHP, flipchart or Velcro board, by Steve Hutchinson*

This talk works best if you feel confident enough to draw the pictures as you go along (which is easier if you draw faint pencil lines in advance). Each picture is turned upside down to become a different image for the next part of the talk.

Introduce the talk by saying that the Christmas story is full of people who were surprised.

**1 Joseph was surprised**

Mary, Joseph's true love, had promised to marry him. But he was worried and sad. *(Draw his head the sad way up.)*

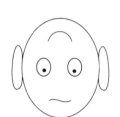

Mary was pregnant. Then Joseph had a dream. It was a surprising dream because God spoke to him.

But it was also a fantastic dream because now he understood what was happening! God turned Joseph's thinking upside down. *(Turn the head upside down to show that Joseph is happy.)*

**2 The shepherds were surprised**

It was a quiet night. The sheep and shepherds were on the hillside above Bethlehem. The shepherds were used to being out all night with their sheep. *(Draw some sheep: clouds with triangle faces and stick legs.)*

Suddenly, their world was turned upside down and they were very surprised and terribly afraid!
*(Turn upside down and make triangles into angels with heads and wings.)*

An angel appeared telling them not to be afraid. 'I've got good news,' he said. 'It will bring great joy to everyone.'

Joy: that would be a surprise for some people! A chance to be really happy! Lots of people would like true happiness.

8

### 3 The wise men were surprised

The wise men came looking for a baby, born as king of the Jews. *(Draw a crown.)*

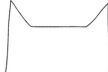

They went to King Herod's palace first. He was very surprised and upset at the news. 'I'm the king of the Jews,' he said. There was no baby there.

So they followed the star that they had seen at the start. It went ahead of them until it stopped over the place where the child was. They went in... and had a surprise! *(Turn the crown upside down and draw in a baby.)*

No crown, but a baby! Thirty years ago on Christmas Eve, a young man sat in a churchyard, wondering about God. He was half atheist (meaning he didn't believe in God) and half agnostic (meaning he didn't know). He said to God, 'If you are real, show yourself to me.' God turned his life upside down. He is the Right Reverend Jim Thompson, now Bishop of Bath and Wells. *(You could also include here the story of someone you know whose life has been turned upside down since they became a Christian.)*

Perhaps the biggest surprise of all is that God chose to come to earth as a vulnerable baby because of his great love for us.

The angel said, 'Your Saviour is born.' Here is someone who will turn your life upside down. He can completely change you and give you real happiness... if you will let him.

Will you tell him you love him? Will you ask him into your life to change you? You may be in for a big surprise!

## No wrapping

*A short talk, by Vicki Blyth*

**You will need:** *three similar sized boxes, wrapping paper, an image of a cross or an actual wooden cross, concertina-folded paper with the word LIFE cut out so as to make a string of letters, a sack or bag to put presents in*

Make up the following three presents using the boxes. Present 1 contains junk but is beautifully wrapped; present 2 contains the cross and is plainly wrapped, and present 3 contains the string of letters.

Take present 1 from your sack or bag. As you take off the wrapping, comment on how beautiful the wrapping is and then express shock and disappointment when you see what is inside. Relate this to the way we often have junk in our lives that we would rather hide away, but when we do get a glimpse of it, we can be shocked and disappointed.

Take present 2 from your sack or bag and open it. Comment on it being a rather unusual gift. Explain that the cross represents salvation and the fact that God sent his Son to get rid of our clutter and give us the best present we could ever hope for. Say how it was not neatly packaged, with sparkly glitter and fancy bits of ribbon. It was gruesome and painful, but means we can have...

Now open present 3 and reveal the string of LIFE – and as you do so say the words 'eternal life' to complete the talk.

# Operation Christmas Child

*An all-age community event for November to give to needy children overseas*

## Background information

Samaritan's Purse is an international relief agency that aims to meet the critical needs of victims of war, poverty, famine, disease, and natural disaster, while sharing the good news of Jesus Christ. Through 'Operation Christmas Child' they offer a message of hope to children in desperate situations around the world, by sending them gift-filled shoeboxes. The gifts are given regardless of nationality, ethnic or political background or religious beliefs, to children requiring nothing of them, their families or the communities in return. Wherever it is culturally appropriate and in partnership with local agents, children are given a booklet with Bible stories in their own language.

With the help of thousands of volunteers, Samaritan's Purse collects and processes these gift-filled shoeboxes in its warehouses across the UK. Then, working with national churches and charities, Samaritan's Purse delivers the gifts to children in hospitals, orphanages, IDP camps, homeless shelters, and impoverished neighbourhoods.

For further information, visit:
**www.samaritanspurse.uk.com**

## The aim

To encourage people of all ages to do something practical that will help poor and needy children in other countries but that will also be an opportunity to enjoy some time together and to build relationships. Filling shoeboxes could be done individually but, making it into a community event, is much more fun!

## In advance

Contact Samaritan's Purse to obtain a supply of donations envelopes, gift labels and leaflets on how to pack boxes and what to put in them. There is also some promotional material available such as posters and booklets, as well as DVDs with both short and long presentations that you could use on the day. Stories and PowerPoint presentations are also available on the website: www.samaritanspurse.uk.com

Advertise the need for people to provide gifts, medium-size shoeboxes and wrapping paper in advance of your event, letting them know when and where to deliver these. You may want to have regular collection times and allocate people to be at the venue to receive the items. Collection doesn't necessarily have to be at your church venue, especially if you are not centrally placed in your community. You might find that schools or other churches are happy to help with the collection and storage of the items.

Make sure you include information about what are suitable items for packing in your shoeboxes and what are not. You could also encourage those who are gifted at knitting to knit mittens, scarves or even hand puppets as their contribution! Patterns for clown or teddy bear hand puppets are available on the Samaritan's Purse website.

Set a suitable date for your event. You could make this National Shoebox Sunday (visit www.samaritanspurse.uk.com to find out when this is) or you could pack the boxes prior to this and celebrate all you have achieved on National Shoebox Sunday. Whatever you decide to do, bear in mind boxes need to be taken to any of the Samaritan's Purse Drop-Off Points in the first few weeks of November.

Advertise everything about the event in as many places as possible. You could put up posters in places like schools, local community halls, libraries, and public notice boards or get members of your congregation to distribute leaflets.

Ask for a few volunteers to help set up, clear away and count the boxes on the day or to help with catering.

## On the day

Before everyone arrives get your volunteers to help set out enough tables for people to stand at to pack the boxes, with enough room to move around. You may like to have an area where there are smaller tables for children to work at. Distribute wrapping paper, scissors, sticky tape, shoeboxes, gift labels, and pens on each table. Have a recycling bag available for unwanted wrapping paper, and also someone to take care of a collection bag or pot for people to put in their £2 donation (see below for more details). Alternatively, if you have the facility to set up a computer, you could pay for the shoe boxes online and the receipt can be printed and put in the box. Put the gifts on a separate table for people to select the right items for their box. If you have a lot of gifts you may like to arrange them under themes such as toys, practical items, clothes, and so on.

## Presentation

As people arrive you might like to do a short presentation explaining about 'Operation Christmas Child' or you could ask for a registered volunteer from Samaritan's Purse to come in and speak about it. Thank everyone for coming then explain how to fill each box as described on the leaflets or on the website. (Go to **www.samaritanspurse.uk.com** and click on 'Filling a box'.) Or if you prefer you can print out the web page and distribute several copies across the tables for people to follow. Explain about the £2 donation that is required by Samaritan's Purse to cover distribution, transport, processing and promotion costs.

You could give them the choice to contribute or not, but you will need to make up the deficit. Encourage the children to take part in the decision-making process of what to put in the boxes. You may like to include some secular Christmas music in the background for a relaxed atmosphere.

## Refreshments

You may like to eat together either part way through the session or at the end. It could be a simple meal such as soup and bread or something more ambitious, if you have the time and resources to provide this. If you are not providing food make sure there is an endless supply of drinks available!

## Finishing off

People need to feel free to stay as long as they want to, so do not worry if all your boxes are not completed in the time you have allowed! Ask your volunteers to clear away wrapping paper, scissors and so on, and to put all the filled boxes together to be counted at the end. Fill in the leaflet supplied by Samaritan's Purse with the correct donation for the number of boxes (allow £2 per box). Arrange for the boxes to be taken to the nearest drop-off point in your area before the closing date. (Go to www.samaritanspurse.uk.com and type in your postcode to find out where this is.)

## After the event

For those who are interested there is the opportunity to visit their local Samaritan's Purse warehouse or they could even become a volunteer. For more information visit the website.

You may like to make this a regular event each November. You could take photographs of this year's event and ask people to write down comments on what they thought of the day. Using these items, create an eye-catching information board to put up next year to encourage more people to get involved.

# The people's nativity

*An outdoor performance for the local community, adapted from an original idea by Jane Wade*

## Aim

This event is a great opportunity to bring churches and community together to explore the Christmas story in an innovative way. The idea is to achieve a 'true to life' setting for performing the nativity story, such as a barn or other farm building. If this isn't possible, you could build a stage set to represent the place where Jesus was born, on a village green or another large area where all the community can convene.

## Planning

For this event to work well, you will need to do a lot of planning, about six months in advance. Set up a meeting with all those who wish to be involved in some way. People will be needed to find a suitable venue and have permission to use it, check on any health and safety issues, provide portable toilets, marshal the audience, raise funds, design and make costumes, provide sound and lighting, act, sing, produce and direct. Decide how many performances you want to do and when (you could do one afternoon and one evening performance, for example) and what you want to charge people to come. You could provide tickets to buy in advance.

## Venue

Once you have found the venue, you will need to prepare the site for the performances. If you are using a farm building for instance, you may need to put down gravel to form a path, provide lighting and set up portable toilets. If you are using the village green you will need to write to the Police and Parish Council to ask permission to go ahead and check on traffic flow, safety issues and parking facilities. The 'stable' could be built using pieces of old wood, such as fencing panels.

## Fund-raising

If you want to have professional sound and lighting it will cost around £1,000. It is important that people are able to hear the narration clearly and to see what is going on as it will be dark if you perform in the evening. The lighting also adds atmosphere to specific scenes. Fund-raising events can be great fun and you can involve lots of people in this.

## Costumes

You will need a committed team to set about making the costumes for the actors. To achieve an authentic look, do some research at the library, or by using a web search engine on what they wore at the time of Jesus' birth. Start making a collection of old sheets or items from dressing-up boxes and consider dying them to get the right colour effect.

## Publicity

It is vital you publicise the event widely. Design posters and invitations and ask your local paper if they would like to do a write-up and take photographs.

## Rehearsals

If you want the play to look really professional, start weekly rehearsals from about September onwards. Some weeks you could rehearse specific scenes so not everyone has to turn up each week. The cast includes two narrators – one male and one female for voice variation, Joseph and Mary, an innkeeper and child, four angels, three shepherds, Herod and his assistants, and three wise men. Why not have a real young couple with a new baby to take the part of Mary, Joseph and Jesus? If you do, put a hot water bottle under the blanket in the manger to keep the baby warm!

## On the night

If your farm is quite isolated and parking is restricted you could run a 'park and ride' scheme from various pick-up points around the parishes. You could have marshals in costume to welcome people aboard and you could give your coach a name such as the 'Bethlehem Express'. Get the whole site risk-assessed and provide numerous marshals at the venue, also in costume, to direct people where to go.

## The performance!

Advise people to wrap up warm and wear sensible footwear. Use donkeys, sheep and horses for the wise men as it's unlikely you'll get hold of a camel! Each scene can take place in a different area of the farm so encourage the audience to move around from scene to scene. You can also include some music, dance and singing, to add variety to the performance.

## After the event

Make sure there are plenty of people available to clear up after the event and get things back to normal. This event needs plenty of planning, enthusiasm and hard work, but you will find the experience very enjoyable; people will be brought together and the nativity story will come alive afresh.

12

# The people's nativity

*By Margot Haley and Jane Wade, 2002*

**Characters:** two narrators, Joseph and Mary, innkeeper, a palace guard, four angels, three shepherds, Herod and three wise men

## Act 1

**Bible reading:** John 1:1–5,9–14
*(Read as an opening dramatic reading.)*

**Narrator 1:** In the beginning God created a perfect world and Jesus was there by his side. Jesus is the Word, and he was with God and was truly God. From the very beginning Jesus was with God. And with Jesus, God created all things. Nothing was made without the Word. Everything that was created received its life from him, and his life gave light to everyone.

Men and women were made in the likeness of God, and were given the freedom to make choices in how they lived their lives. Mankind went their own way, choosing deeds of darkness and not light. Jesus came to shine into the darkness. His light keeps shining in the dark, and darkness has never put it out. The True Light that shines on everyone was coming into our world. Jesus came into his own world but his own nation did not welcome him. *(Pause.)* Yet some people accepted him and put their faith in him. So Jesus gave them the right to be the children of God. They were not God's children by nature or because of any human desire or effort. God himself was the one who made them his children. The Word, Jesus, became a human being and lived here with us. We saw his true glory, the glory of the only Son of the Father. From him all the kindness and all the truth of God have come down to us.

**The birth of Jesus:** Matthew 1:18–21
*(Angel and Joseph tableau.)*

**Narrator 1:** This is how Jesus Christ was born. A young woman named Mary was engaged to Joseph, a descendant of King David. But before they were married, she learnt that she was going to have a baby, not by man, but by God's Holy Spirit. Joseph was a good man and did not want to embarrass Mary in front of everyone. So he decided to call off the wedding quietly. While Joseph was thinking about this, an angel from the Lord came to him in a dream. The angel said, 'Joseph, the baby that Mary will have is from the Holy Spirit. Go ahead and marry her. Then after the baby is born name him Jesus, because he will save his people from their sins.'

*(Joseph moves to the donkey; Mary and Joseph start to move to the next area.)*

**Census:** Luke 2:1–4

**Narrator 2:** About that time Emperor Augustus gave orders for the names of all the people in the towns to be listed in record books. These first records were made when Quirinius was governor of Syria. Everyone had to go to his or her own hometown to be listed. So Joseph had to leave Nazareth in Galilee and go to Bethlehem in Judea. Long ago, Bethlehem had been King David's hometown, and Joseph went there because he was from David's family. Mary travelled with Joseph; she was soon to have a baby.

*(Joseph and Mary arrive – they knock on innkeepers' doors or walls. (Interactive speech from Joseph and Mary – improvise! Mary shows stress! Baby is due!)*

**Narrator 1:** Mary and Joseph knocked on the doors of places where they could possibly stay, but without success. *(Mary and Joseph talk.)* But one kindly innkeeper had a place where his animals were kept, where they could stay the night. Mary and Joseph were grateful, and went inside.

*(Innkeeper shows Mary and Joseph to the stable.)*

*(Musical interlude – star to light up, manger moved forward to centre stage.)*

**Narrator 2:** Mary gave birth to her firstborn son, and wrapped him in strips of cloth, and laid him in a manger.

*(Dim lighting in the stable.)*

# Act 2

**Shepherds scene:** Luke 2:8–20
*(General chatter of shepherds.)*

**Narrator 1:** That night in the fields near Bethlehem some shepherds were guarding their sheep.

*(Spot on Angel and flashing lights.)*

All at once an angel came down to them from the Lord, and the brightness of the Lord's glory flashed around them. The shepherds were frightened, but the angel said, 'Don't be afraid! I have good news for you, which will make everyone happy. This very day in Bethlehem, King David's hometown, a Saviour was born for you. He is Christ the Lord. You will know who he is because you will find him wrapped in strips of cloth and lying on a bed of hay.'

*(Other angels appear.)*

Suddenly many other angels came down from heaven and joined in praising God. They said, 'Praise God in heaven! Peace on earth to everyone who pleases God.'

After the angels had left and gone back to heaven, the shepherds said to each other, 'Let's go to Bethlehem and see what the Lord has told us about.'

*(Interaction between shepherds – long pause.)*

*(Shepherds mingle with the audience looking for the still dimmed stable.)*

They hurried off and found Mary and Joseph, and they saw the baby lying on a bed of hay.

*(Stable lighting increased.)*

**Narrator 2:** When the shepherds saw Jesus they told his parents what the angel had said about him. Everyone listened and was surprised. But Mary kept thinking about all this and wondered what it meant.

As the shepherds returned to their sheep they were praising God and saying wonderful things about him to everyone they met.

Everything they had seen and heard was just as the angel had said.

*(During this narration the shepherds will act out the storyline.)*

*(Starlight dims and goes out.)*

*(Wise men start to move.)*

# Act 3

**The wise men:** Matthew 2:1–12
*(The wise men seek Jesus.)*

**Narrator 2:** After Jesus was born in Bethlehem, during the reign of King Herod, three wise men from the East came to Jerusalem seeking the child, born to be King of the Jews.

*(Interactive conversation amongst the wise men – on the fact that they have followed the star from the east – the star being the sign of a newborn king.)*

**Wise man 1:** That looks like Jerusalem ahead.

**Wise man 2:** Yes, Jerusalem – I wonder if the star will stop there.

**Wise man 3:** It seems a likely place to find this new King of the Jews.

**Wise man 3:** That looks like a palace ahead; let's see if anyone there can help us.

*(Palace guard stands at entrance of palace. He moves as if to challenge the wise men.)*

**Wise man 2:** *(To guard.)* We are wise men from the East; we've travelled many miles following a star, and we are looking for the child born to be king of the Jews.

**Palace guard:** Wait here while I speak to the King.

*(Guard moves off stage.)*

**Narrator 1:** When King Herod heard about the arrival of the wise men he was worried, and asked his chief priests and advisors where the Messiah was to be born. He was told that the child would be born in Bethlehem, as the prophets had foretold. So Herod asked to see the wise men.

*(Guard signals for wise men to enter. Wise men move to Herod on his throne to converse.)*

**Narrator 1:** Herod told the wise men to search carefully for the child and to let him know when they had found him, so that he could go and worship the child himself.

*(Herod moves off stage.)*

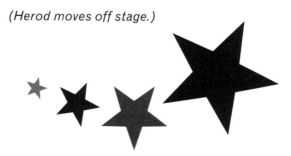

## Act 4

*(Wise men turn and see the star – star to light up. Interactive conversation between the wise men, as they make their way to the stable, following the star.)*

**Wise man 1:** There's the star! That must be the way to Bethlehem.

**Wise man 3:** What did you make of Herod?

**Wise man 2:** I'm not sure. I can't see a tyrant like him worshipping another King.

**Wise man 3:** Especially a baby!

**Wise man 1:** The star has stopped over that stable, can that be right?

**Wise man 2:** Only one way to find out.

*(Pause as they look.)*

**Wise man 3:** The baby's here!

**Narrator 2:** The wise men brought the infant child, Jesus, gifts of gold, frankincense and myrrh. They knelt down and worshipped him. *(Giving of gifts.)* God warned the wise men in a dream not to return to Herod, so they travelled home another way.

## Act 5

*(Final scene – shepherds and wise men come to the front. Mary and Joseph, with baby, take centre stage, with everyone else grouped around them.)*

## Song

All sing: 'Silent Night' (including the audience).

# Shepherds and angels party

*Ideas for a themed party for children*

The aim of this party is for children to have lots of fun and spend time with friends, while at the same time helping them to think a bit more about the Christmas story.

## Invitations

Make sure every child in your group receives an invitation several weeks in advance of the event. Copy the invitation on page 18 onto brightly coloured card and fill in the details of your party.

## Dressing up

Encourage the guests and leaders to wear a shepherd or angel outfit. For those who do not like dressing up they could always bring along a toy sheep!

## Prizes

Some of the games will have one or more winners. Keep the prizes very small and inexpensive, for example, pencils, rubbers, sweets. You could go to your local Christian bookshop for stickers of sheep or angels to fit the theme!

## Party food

If you intend to provide food, drinks or sweets, ask parents in advance for written consent and a note of any allergies or items that they do not want their child to be given. To continue the shepherds and angels theme you might like to consider having shepherd's pie and angel cakes! (See recipe for angel cakes on page 92.)

## Face-painting

Have a face-painting table where an adult paints on beards, bushy eyebrows and rosy cheeks for shepherds, and glittery shapes or swirls for the angels.

## Starting off

It's always a good idea to have an activity for children to do as soon as they arrive at a party. This will keep the early ones busy until everyone has arrived and you're ready to play your first game. You could use one or both of the following craft activities. The angel mobile is more suitable for older children to make. When the children have completed these you could hang them up around the room as decorations for the party.

## Concertina angels

**You will need:** *collage materials such as doilies, silver or gold paper, lace, tinsel, sequins and glitter, a template of an angel (see page 80)*

Tape together several sheets of A4 paper lengthways to make a long strip. Fold in concertina style (A5 size) and draw a bold angel shape on the top fold. Make sure the arms and robe extend right to the edge of the page.

Cut round the angel shape, so that when unfolded, there are several angels joined to each other. (Have sticky tape ready for emergency repairs!) Decorate the angels with the collage materials. Try and make them 'shine' with the glory of God!

Write the child's name on the back of the decoration so they can easily identify it to take home at the end of the party, and then hang it up as decoration for the party.

## Angel mobile

**You will need:** *templates from page 80, wire coat hangers (one each), tinsel, cards, tissue paper, glitter, thread, hole punch, pens, scissors, sticky tape, glue*

Cover the coat hanger with tinsel.

Make a stencil of the angel shape from the template, cut out an angel shape, add a face and decorate it.

For each angel, cut six bell shapes out of tissue paper. Put these together over the angel's skirt, and staple in the middle as shown in the diagram. Separate the individual layers of skirt to make a 3D angel.

Punch a hole near the top of each angel and hang from your coat hanger mobile.

# Games

Depending on the age group of the children at your party, choose from these games ideas:

## Sheep and shepherds

This game is based on 'What's the time, Mr Wolf?' and is suitable for younger children.

Explain the rules of the game. Choose a child to be the 'shepherd' and ask them to walk around the room with the 'sheep' following behind.

As they walk, the sheep ask, 'What's the time, Mr Shepherd?' The shepherd turns round and answers:

Feeding time! *(Sheep pretend to eat.)*
Sleeping time! *(Sheep lie down.)*
Counting time! *(Sheep stand in a line.)*
Shearing time! *(Sheep scatter – the last one caught becomes the next shepherd.)*

## Pin the tail on the sheep

Play a variation of the game 'Pin the tail on the donkey'. Have a large picture of a sheep without his tail. Have a separate tail made of strips of wool bound together with a blob of Blu-tack on the back. Blindfold the children, one at a time, and turn them round three times before standing them in front of the picture and letting them attempt to fix the tail to the right place. Award a prize to the child who comes the nearest to the spot.

## Race to the manger

This game is suitable for all ages (and great fun if adults take part too!). It is also a way of including the Christmas story at your party.

Sit in a circle. Explain that you will be telling part of the Christmas story and that everyone will be given the name of a character. Whenever they hear that name, they should stand up, run around the group and back to their place in a clockwise direction. Say that when you say 'all the people' everyone should run round!

Allocate the following names to different individuals: shepherds, angel, heaven's angels, Jesus, God, Mary, and Joseph.

Read the following story, pausing to allow the runners to return to their places.

While **Mary** and **Joseph** watched over the sleeping baby **Jesus** in a stable in Bethlehem, there were some **shepherds** who were spending the night in their fields, taking care of their sheep. An **angel** of the Lord appeared and the glory of **God** appeared all around them. They were really scared, but the **angel** said to them,

'Don't be afraid! I am here with good news for you, which will bring joy to all the people. Today, in Bethlehem, your Saviour has been born. His name is **Jesus**. You will recognise **Jesus** because he is wrapped in swaddling clothes and lying in a manger.

Suddenly an army of **heaven's angels** appeared with the **angel**, singing praises to God: 'Glory to **God** in the highest heaven and peace on earth to those with whom he is pleased!'

When the **angels** went back to heaven, the **shepherds** said to each other, 'Let's go to Bethlehem and see this **Jesus**, whom God has told us about.'

So they hurried off and found **Mary** and **Joseph** and saw **Jesus** lying in the manger. When the **shepherds** saw him, they told **Mary** and **Joseph** what the **angel** had said about the child. **Mary** and **Joseph** were amazed at what the **shepherds** said.

**Mary** remembered all these things and thought about them. The **shepherds** went back, singing praises to **God** for all they had heard and seen – it had been just as the **angel** had told them.

## Memory game

Have a tray full of items that follow the theme of angels and shepherds. Explain that the children need to try and memorise as many items as possible on the tray. You could include items such as an angel tree decoration or a Christmas card depicting an angel, a toy trumpet or another instrument, a packet of Angel Delight, a toy sheep, woollen socks, a whistle, a tea towel, a chunk of cheese, a bottle of water, a packet of crisps, a torch, a box of matches, a book of jokes, a pipe cleaner in the shape of a crook. Give the children five minutes to look at everything on the tray, then take it away and give out paper and pens for them to write down as many things they can remember. Give a prize to the child with the highest score.

## Sheep search

**You will need:** *sheep shapes made from card, each with one word on it from the following verse: 'This very day in David's town your Saviour was born!' Luke 2:11 (GNB)*

Hide the sheep shapes around the room. Tell the children that a shepherd has lost all his sheep and they are hidden all over the room. Encourage the children to search for the sheep and bring them back to a central point.

Turn the shapes over to find the words and help the group to put the words in order so that they make up the Bible verse.

# Shepherds and angels party

_____

is invited to a Christmas party

Date_____

Time_____

Place_____

Please dress up as an angel or a shepherd!

## Promises

*An Advent talk based on Luke 1:67–79*

**You will need:** *one very large chocolate bar, five regular-sized chocolate bars of the same kind*

Before the service, place the chocolate bars somewhere concealed, but accessible, at the front of the room.

Ask if anyone would like some chocolate – there will undoubtedly be lots of volunteers! Point out that everyone is assuming that you do actually have chocolate to give out, but reassure prospective volunteers by promising that there will be chocolate for whoever is chosen. Choose someone to come and receive the chocolate. Give him or her all five of the regular-sized chocolate bars. Ask how it feels! Ask whether there is anyone else who would still like some chocolate. Suggest that the volunteer with the five bars of chocolate gives one to someone else. (They will probably be quite happy to do this.) Continue the pattern of asking who else would like chocolate and suggesting that your volunteer gives one of their bars away. You will probably discover that they find it increasingly hard to part with the chocolate – especially when there's only one bar left (so that giving it away would leave them with nothing).

If your volunteer would rather not give away their last bar, don't condemn them – their decision is perfectly understandable! However, do ask everyone to suggest what the reasons behind the volunteer's decision might be. It will probably emerge that they feared being left with nothing for themselves. Once this is established ask if anyone can remember what you said at the start. You promised there would be chocolate for whoever was chosen to come forward. Now produce the giant chocolate bar and say that this was waiting for the volunteer if they had given away their last bar. (It can be shared out later, if it has not been given to the volunteer.) Ask the volunteer how he or she would have felt about receiving the giant chocolate bar. They will probably suggest feelings of joy and delight.

Link the sense of joy and delight with Zechariah's song of joy and delight in Luke 1:67–79 in response to the birth of his son, John. Draw attention to the 'promise' being a central theme of Zechariah's song. John's birth not only shows that God has kept his promise of a child to Zechariah and Elizabeth, but it also shows God at work, keeping a much older promise to his people to send help to them (verses 70 and 72). Zechariah was singing about John getting everything ready for Jesus' arrival. Zechariah was happy because God was keeping his promises.

The chocolate activity illustrates how quickly we can forget promises, or how we can become used to not being able to trust people to keep their promises. However, as the Bible passage shows, we can be confident that God does keep his promises – even if we have to wait a long time to see it happen.

In the unlikely event that the volunteer did part with all five chocolate bars, simply adapt this talk to focus on confidence in the promise that there would be chocolate for them. Use their confidence as an example to others, of the confidence we can have in God's promises. Then give the volunteer the giant chocolate bar and compare their joy at receiving it with Zechariah's joy at seeing God keep his promises.

## Give and receive

*Preparing for Christmas*

**You will need:** *a card copy of the Shepherd Christmas card from page 23 for each person, paper and pens, mince pies or foil-wrapped biscuits, an open decorative box*

Place the Christmas cards at the front along with the mince pies or foil-wrapped biscuits.

Give everyone a sheet of paper and a pen. Ask for a show of hands of how many people have made a Christmas gift list? We give gifts to celebrate the coming of Christ. What gifts might we give to Christ this Christmas so that we can make him the centre of our celebrations? Ask everyone to write or draw on their sheet of paper something that they can give to Jesus this Christmas. For adults this might be more time in prayer, or more attention to Bible reading. For children it might be more about listening to parents or carers, or sharing their toys.

Lead the congregation in this simple prayer of dedication:
'Thank you for all the preparations we are able to make to celebrate the coming of Christ this Christmas. Help us not to forget to prepare our hearts as well as our homes. We ask you to make our hearts and lives clean and ready for Jesus. May we give you time and space and love this Christmas. Equip us for making Christ the centre of our Christmas. Amen.'

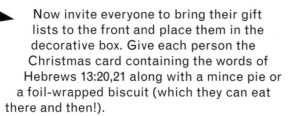

Now invite everyone to bring their gift lists to the front and place them in the decorative box. Give each person the Christmas card containing the words of Hebrews 13:20,21 along with a mince pie or a foil-wrapped biscuit (which they can eat there and then!).

## The perfect Christmas?

*Challenging people of all ages to think of what Christmas is all about*

**You will need:** *a PowerPoint presentation, OHP slides or flip chart with a list of Christmas 'problems' as shown below, a small consolation prize (optional)*

Display a list of predictable things that might have happened to a family in the run-up to Christmas. Divide into families or groups of three or four. Ask each group to keep a total of how many of these things have happened to one or more of them this year:

1 Christmas tree bulbs blown
2 A hidden present discovered
3 Items of food not obtained
4 Unexpected visitors
5 Family squabbles
6 Outrageous gift requests
7 Cards received from someone you don't know
8 Dull Christmas newsletters to read in full
9 Missed something good on TV
10 Watched something bad on TV

Applaud the family or group with the highest score and maybe award them a small consolation prize.

Remind everyone that if they think they have had a lot of problems to overcome this Christmas, we should remember what the run-up to the first Christmas must have been like for Mary and Joseph. Review the key points of the nativity story, highlighting the potential problems such as an unplanned pregnancy, the journey to Bethlehem near Mary's due date, no room at the inn and giving birth in a cattle shed. Explain that this Christmas you're encouraging everyone to give thanks to God that, despite all this, the birth of Jesus was the best gift that God could ever give to his people.

## Christmas card exchange

*A talk based on Luke 2:17–19 reflecting on the wonder of the Christmas message*

**You will need:** *a copy for each person of the 'Wow' Christmas card on page 24 (copied onto card), pens, pencils, colouring materials, a large box*

Prepare enough copies (on card) of the template for everyone to have one. Fold each one in half to form a Christmas card with the 'Wow' flash on the front.

Read Luke 2:17–19. Say that, like Mary, we should keep on thinking about God's goodness in sending Jesus and wondering what that means for us each day. To help with this you're going to exchange Christmas cards!

Give everyone a card and a pen or pencil. Ask everyone to spend a few moments thinking about today's Bible passage and the 'Wow' factor in it. They should then write or draw (and colour) inside their cards one thing about the story that makes them think, 'Wow!' All the cards should then be brought to the front and placed in the large box (or the box could be passed around if you prefer). Everyone should then be invited to pick out a card from the box at random. *(If by chance they pick their own they should replace it and choose another one.)* They can take the cards home to serve as a constant reminder of the Christmas 'Wow' factor and God's goodness in sending Jesus.

## Gold, incense, myrrh

*Learning the meaning of the gifts brought to Jesus*

**You will need:** *some gold items (for example, jewellery), incense and perfume*

Ask for examples of items made of gold. Most will be jewellery although there may be some people who have gold in a watch mechanism or in their teeth.

Show the gold items you have brought. Explain that gold has long been associated with luxury and kingship. There was a lot of gold in King Solomon's temple. Read 2 Chronicles 4:7,8. The wise men brought gold to Jesus because he was a descendant of King David and was himself a special sort of king.

Ask for examples of incense in today's world. The most familiar equivalent for many people today might be joss sticks, often used to make a room smell good. Show the incense item you have brought and, if it is something you can light, do so.

Read Exodus 30:34–36. Explain that frankincense has long been associated with worship and Moses was instructed to use it as part of a recipe for the most holy of incenses. The wise men brought frankincense to Jesus because he was worthy of worship.

Ask for examples of myrrh in today's world. People may mention drugs, possibly perfume. Show the perfume you have brought. Invite a few people to comment on the smell.

Read Psalm 45:7,8. Explain that myrrh is associated with riches, healing and embalming the dead and, in this psalm, with the perfumed fragrance of someone wealthy, such as a king. The wise men brought myrrh to Jesus. Perhaps they knew that one day this child, who was a king, would die for his people and be laid in a grave.

You may think these were surprising gifts to bring to a baby, but they were just the right gifts to show that the Christmas baby was really *the King*.

## Timeline

*Understanding the long preparation for the coming of the Saviour*

**You will need:** *four volunteers (three male and one female), enlarged versions of the individual names on page 25 with the appropriate Bible verse on the back of each; a long strip of paper (wallpaper or lining paper is ideal) with the following words spaced at appropriate intervals: 2,000 years to go…1,000 years to go…700 years to go… 9 months to go*

Read Luke 2:1–7. Many of us are not very good at waiting for something we want to happen. Waiting for God to send the promised Saviour took a very long time indeed, but God told them a little bit more about this Saviour as the years went by.

Invite the four volunteers to come forward to help as you begin to unroll your long paper strip. Reveal just the first marker ('2,000 years to go'). This was when God first made a promise to Abraham. *(Give the 'Abraham' sign to the first volunteer and ask him to read the words on the back.)* It was going to be one of Abraham's descendents who would be a blessing to everyone in the world.

Reveal the second marker on the paper roll ('1,000 years to go'). God made another promise, this time to King David. *(Give the 'David' label to the second volunteer and invite him to read the words on the card.)* Explain that David was the greatest king of Israel.

Bethlehem was always known as David's town. When God promised that someone from David's family would always be king, some people expected God's Saviour to be the ruler of Israel, but God was going to send a Saviour for the whole world.

Unroll the third marker and give the 'Isaiah' label to the third volunteer. *(The third volunteer reads from the card.)* After the time of Isaiah, the people were ruled by one foreign king after another. Then, about 700 years later, the question they were asking was, how would God keep his promise when they were ruled by a foreign emperor and not God's chosen king, like David?

When the angel visited Mary, he gave her the most amazing promise of all! *(Unroll the fourth marker, give the 'Mary' label to the last volunteer and ask her to read out the card.)* God had waited until everything was just right to fulfil his promise in the birth of Jesus. Jesus was born to a family who belonged to King David's family line, in Bethlehem, King David's town – but not in a palace – in a stable. He would be a different kind of king!

## Light

*A talk using light based on John 1:1–14*

**You will need:** *an OHP and screen, a large, clear glass bowl (no brand name on the base), cling film, a sheet of card, a dropper and bottles of food colouring (yellow, orange and red), music, a CD player, water*

Have the OHP on a steady table and cover the glass and sides with clear cling film. Half fill the bowl with water and place the card over the top before you begin. If you do not have an OHP, three assistants can hold the bowl, shine a bright torch up through it and handle the cover and colours.

Read John 1:1–5. *(Place the covered bowl of water on the OHP and switch it on. Some light will shine on the screen, though the centre will be dark.)* Say that this visual aid represents 'the light shining in the darkness' (v 5). Explain that these verses introduce the good news about Jesus in John's Gospel. They talk about darkness and light not meaning day and night, but rather explaining about the right and wrong ways of living. God's way is like living in the light, while living any other way is like darkness. Ask everyone to think of situations in the world or in their own lives that have been like darkness. Give a few examples – war, arguments, bullying, meanness, telling lies, letting others down. It might be appropriate to say a prayer of confession at this point.

However, though our lives can be dark with the wrong things we do or bad things that happen to us, the 'darkness has never put it [the light] out' (v 5).

Read John 1:5–9. (*Move the bowl's cover very slightly to show a little more light on the screen.*) God doesn't want us to live in darkness, and so he did something to help us. The first sign that something wonderful was going to happen was the arrival of John the Baptist. He explained that he was not the light himself. He came to help people have faith in God and to show them the way to God – rather like a torch shining on a dark night. He said that someone great was about to come into the world (v 9).

Read John 1:10–13. (*Remove the cover to reveal the light shining through the water.*) The Word, as John called him, was Jesus. And when he came into the world, the light of God shone through him. His way of life was God's way of life and so there was no darkness, no wrongdoing in anything he did or said.

(*Replace the cover.*) But sadly, people did not recognise who he was. It was as though they hid in a dark place instead of enjoying the sunlight. People still do that today. But, if we accept Jesus into our lives, it's like living in the light. (*Remove the cover again.*)

Read John 1:14. (*As you speak, agitate the water and put drops of food colouring on to the surface.*) When Jesus came as a human being, he brought God's light into the world. John uses the word 'glory'. The glory of Jesus is that he shows us exactly what God is like – that God is light. We don't have to live in darkness any more. This means that we can:

- know that God forgives us
- refuse to give in to wrong desires
- head away from paths that lead us into danger and instead come close to God
- be confident about the future.

Give each person (or small group) a clear plastic cup with a little water in it. Ask them to hold their hands around and over the cup and think of one part of their life that is full of darkness – a person they dislike or fear, a situation that is worrying or hopeless, something about themselves that they would like to change. Play some quiet music. Then announce, 'The true light that shines on everyone is coming into the world! All hold up your cups to let the light shine through.' Close by thanking God for the transforming light that Jesus brings us.

# Party invitations

*A talk to emphasise how Jesus came for everyone*

**You will need:** *a selection of newspapers and magazines, scissors, glue, felt-tip pens, two copies of the party scene on page 26 for each person*

Place some of the newspapers and magazines, scissors and glue on tables around the room.

Ask everyone to get into mixed age groups around the craft tables. Ask them to imagine that they're having a party and they can invite whoever they like. They should then look through the newspapers and magazines for pictures of those people they would like to invite. The faces can be cut out and stuck in the appropriate place on one copy of the party scene. Alternatively, they could draw faces of people they know. Invite a selection of people to bring their sheet to the front and tell everyone who they've invited. Talk with them about why they chose those people, highlighting considerations such as who they know, who they like, who they'd like to spend time with or be seen with.

Point out that this is how most people go about deciding who to invite to a party. Then go on to say that when Jesus was born the first people to hear the good news were a bunch of shepherds out in the fields (Luke 2:8–14). Shepherds were very ordinary people, not the kind of people that others wanted to spend much time with or invite to their parties! They lived out in the fields with the sheep, and because they sometimes had to handle dead sheep they would have been thought of as 'unclean'. But these are the people to whom the angels were sent. This tells us something very important – that Jesus is good news for *everyone*. He is not just for those who are attractive or popular, not just for those who are brainy or who always get the promotion, not just for those with money or power – no, he is good news for everyone!

Now ask everyone to take their second copy of the party scene and to imagine that it's a picture of a party to celebrate the birth of Jesus. Given that Jesus came for everyone, who should be at this party? Allow time for everyone to look back through the newspapers and magazines to find images that they think are appropriate to cut out and stick onto this party scene. Again, invite some people to share and talk about the scene they have created.

Encourage everyone to make some time over the next few days to be thankful that Jesus came for everyone.

22

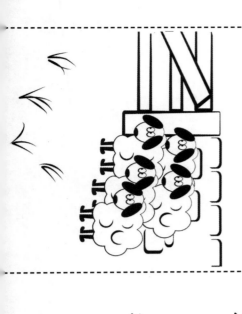

1 Fold down centre line, along 'Fold 1'.

2 Fold end flaps backwards along both 'Fold 2' lines.

3 Turn the card over, and fold the picture ends inwards (along the 'Fold 3' lines) to the centre, so that the pictures match up.

'God gives peace, and he raised our Lord Jesus Christ from death. Now Jesus is like a Great Shepherd whose blood was used to make God's eternal agreement with his flock. I pray that God will make you ready to obey him and that you will always be eager to do right. May Jesus help you do what pleases God. To Jesus Christ be glory for ever and ever.'
(Hebrews 13:20–21)

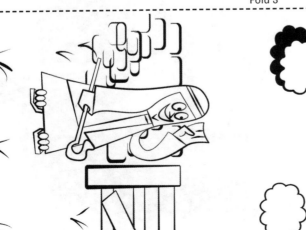

Fold

# Abraham

God said to Abraham:
'You have obeyed me, and so you and your descendants will be a blessing to all nations on earth.'

Genesis 22:18

# King David

God said to David:
'I will make sure that one of your descendants will always be king.'

2 Samuel 7:16

# Isaiah

God said to Isaiah:
'... someone from David's family will some day be king. The Spirit of the Lord will be with him to give him understanding, wisdom and insight.'

Isaiah 11:1,2

# Mary

The angel of God told Mary:
'... you will have a son. His name will be Jesus. He will be great and will be called the Son of God Most High. The Lord God will make him king, as his ancestor David was.'

Luke 1:31,32

# Giving presents

*An assembly outline suitable for Key Stage 1, by Heather Butler*

## Aims

- to make a timeline of the key events in the Christmas story (Luke 2:1–20; Matthew 2:1–12) and think what would go in a cracker to celebrate Jesus' birthday
- to consider what children can give at Christmas time

## You will need

- crackers
- paper and thick felt-tip pens (for drawing)
- large sheets of paper to make the shell of the cracker with some string to tie the cracker up
- cymbals

## Introduction

Open a cracker and look at what is inside: a joke, present, hat, 'crack'. Discuss when crackers are used and why.

## Story

We're going to make a cracker for Jesus' birthday party to help remind us of what happened at Christmas.

*(Take suggestions from the children about what happens in the Christmas story. Draw each suggestion and ask different children to hold each drawing up. Then tell the story, putting the pictures in the correct place to make a timeline.)*

It was nearly time for Mary to have her baby. 'Time to go,' Joseph said.

They had a long journey ahead of them to Bethlehem. That was the village where Joseph had been born and they were going there to pay some money to the Romans. Lots of other people were going there, too.

When they arrived, there was nowhere for them to stay. They were so tired. At last, someone said there was a stable they could use. 'Thank you,' Joseph said.

He helped Mary get off the donkey she had been riding on and made a bed of straw so she could lie down. It wasn't long before there was a baby's cry. Jesus, the Son of God, had come into the world, born in a stable.

Near Bethlehem, some shepherds were looking after their sheep when suddenly there was a great big flash of light and singing in the sky. The shepherds were really scared! Angels appeared, sent from God to tell them about Jesus' birth.

'Let's go and find this Jesus,' they said when the angels left them. So they did. They left their sheep and went down to Bethlehem and found Mary and Joseph and baby Jesus.

Mary and Joseph stayed in Bethlehem for a long time. As soon as there was room they moved out of the stable to a proper house and it was there that some wise men came to visit them bringing gifts of gold, frankincense and myrrh. The gold was to show that Jesus was a king.

*(Draw a crown. Add the motto, a letter to wish Jesus a happy birthday. Either ask the children to make one up or use this one: 'Dear Jesus, happy birthday. Thanks for coming. Love...' Put it with the crown and drawings of the Christmas story.*

*For the 'crack' make a loud bang with a cymbal, then sing a Christmas song like the angels would have done.*

*Lastly, take the children's suggestions as to which presents they could give to Jesus. Draw them and wrap the drawings up in a larger sheet of paper to make the cracker.)*

## Thinking time

The shepherds and the wise men brought presents for Jesus. We too can give presents. What can we give? To whom? Which charities have the children heard of this Christmas?

Christmas is a time for giving. Christians believe it's the time when God gave his son to the world.

## Prayer

Dear God, we've been thinking about some of the people who went to the first Christmas party. They brought presents with them. Thank you that we can give presents as well. Amen.

27

# The light of the world

*An assembly outline suitable for Key Stage 2, by John Hayward*

## Aims

- to think about the significance of light for Christians at Christmas – a festival which is all about the birth of Jesus, the light of the world
- to consider ways in which we can show the qualities of 'light' in our lives

## You will need

- flip chart or similar – the sheet to be divided into two columns – one labelled 'light', the other labelled 'dark'
- note pad and pencil
- Words which fit the categories 'light' or 'dark' (for example: love, peace, kindness, fear, lies, fighting) written clearly on separate strips of card or paper. Include the words 'God' and 'Jesus'. You may like to have some spare strips ready so you can add other words during the assembly
- Blu-tack
- A candle and matches

## Bible base

1 John 1:5; Luke 2:32; John 8:12

## Content

Show the flip chart with the two columns labelled 'light' and 'dark'. Talk about words linked with light and darkness (for example: sunshine, shadows, lightning, night-time). Ask the children for their suggestions and jot them down as a reminder for yourself of what they have said.

Ask them to show you whether they think these words belong in the 'light' or the 'dark' column, in the following way. As you call out the words they have suggested they must either put their hands over their eyes to show the word belongs in the 'dark' column; or flick their hands (open and closed) in front of their eyes to show that the word belongs in the 'light' column.

Introduce another way of thinking about light and darkness. Show the words on the cards you prepared before the assembly (love, fear, and so on...) one at a time. Explain any they don't understand. Ask the children which column each card belongs in and then stick it in the appropriate place, using Blu-tack.

Explain that Christians believe that 'God' should go in the 'light' section because the Bible says: 'God is light, and in him there is no darkness at all.' (1 John 1:5, NCV) Ask the

children if they agree with this. Talk about Jesus, 'the light of the world'.

Explain that at Christmas time, Christians celebrate the birth of Jesus. The Bible says that when Jesus was six weeks old, Mary and Joseph took him to the temple in Jerusalem to dedicate him to God because that was the custom of his people.

There was an old man in the temple called Simeon. When he saw Jesus, he took him in his arms. He said that Jesus would be a light for the people to see (Luke 2:32).

When he grew up, Jesus said, 'I am the light of the world. The person who follows me will never live in darkness' (John 8:12, NCV).

The Bible shows that Jesus was a man who was loving and kind, a good man who helped people and spoke the truth, a man of joy and peace. *(You could remind the children of some examples from Jesus' life.)*

If the children think these things written about Jesus are true, which side of the chart should 'Jesus' go on? Christians believe that Jesus always showed these qualities of 'light' in his life and never those of 'darkness'.

## Application

Light is special for Christians at Christmas time, as they celebrate his birth, because they remember the qualities of 'light' lived out by Jesus. Christians believe that following Jesus brings these qualities of 'light' out in their lives as well.

Look at the words you have stuck in the 'light' column. Ask the children which qualities of light others might see in them.

## Response

Light the candle. Ask the children: 'If you go into a dark room and turn on the light, what happens to the darkness? Does the darkness ever put out the light?' Christians believe that these qualities of 'light' are 'stronger' than the things that are on the 'dark' side, just like light is 'stronger' than darkness.

Look again at the words on the 'light' side. Ask the children to think about situations where they might be able to show 'light' in the darkness.

The light of the world

Assemblies

28

# Gifts

*An assembly outline suitable for Key Stage 3, by Wayne Dixon*

## Bible base

Matthew 2:11; John 3:16

## Aim

- to encourage students to remember that the reason for Christmas and presents is to celebrate the birthday of Jesus, God's gift to the world

## You will need

- party hat, large birthday badge (for example, '18 today')
- five or six 'presents', for example, small bags of sweets (optional, see 'Note')
- CD which the age group would enjoy for a party
- bag of crisps
- can of drink
- CD of the carol you plan to use
- equipment to play the CDs

## Preparation

Before the assembly, wrap up the 'presents'.

Set up the equipment for playing the CD in the assembly, and make sure it all works.

Before the assembly, enlist the help of four or five volunteers and give them one of the 'presents'. Explain briefly that you are going to invite them to bring their 'present' to the front, and then to act as if they are enjoying a party. You will tell them what to do as the assembly progresses. You might like to ask the teacher responsible for the assembly to select 'appropriate' volunteers for you. See 'Note' at end of outline (optional).

## Presentation

Start by talking about parties. Find out:

- are they going to any parties this Christmas?
- have they been to or had any good birthday parties?

Say that you want them to imagine how they would feel if the following happened at their birthday party.

Ask students to imagine that it is their birthday. *(Put on a party hat yourself, and a badge with '18 today' at this point.)*

You are going to have a party. You invite your friends and they are all going to come. The food and drink look great. *(Bring out a token bag of*

crisps and a can of drink!)*

It's all ready. Everyone comes. *(At this point, invite your 'party guests' to come to the front carrying their presents. Play the CD, keeping the volume low, so you can be heard. Encourage your volunteers to act as if they are at a party.)*

Say that all is going well. You notice that they've each brought a present with them – and you think, 'Great – I wonder what I've got!'

Then the music stops. *(Turn off the music.)*

People start getting out their presents. *(Encourage your 'party guests' to look at their presents.)*

You wait for them to give you the presents – after all, it is *your* birthday. *(Look excited!)*

But they do not. Your friends give each other the presents! *(Encourage your 'party guests' to give one another the presents and to unwrap them, dropping the paper on the floor, leaving you out.)*

Ask: 'How would you feel if this was your party?'

*(Thank your volunteers and ask them to go back to their places.)*

Say that the party is over. All your friends have gone and you have been left on your own with just the wrappings.

## Reflection

Say that maybe that's how Jesus feels about Christmas. Briefly comment on how there's lots of partying at Christmas. Then ask about the actual meaning of Christmas, 'Whose birthday is it anyway?'

Talk about how today we often forget that Christmas is about celebrating Jesus' birthday. We get preoccupied with thinking about the presents we're going to give to other people, and what we're going to get. This is a contrast to the first Christmas when Jesus was the centre of attention and three very special gifts were given to the baby. Briefly explain that gold was for a king, frankincense for a priest and that myrrh, used in burial customs, reminds us of Jesus' death.

Explain that Christians started giving gifts to each other at Christmas as a reminder and celebration of God's gift of Jesus to the world.

At this point, you could read John 3:16 from the Bible.

## Response

In a time of quiet:

Ask the students to think about the presents they plan to give, and the ones they hope to get. Encourage them to let every present this Christmas be a reminder of how God showed his love for us, through his gift of Jesus to the world.

Thank God for sending Jesus into the world for us.

Ask the students if they can think of someone who is going to be left out of Christmas celebrations this year. Is there something they could do, or a gift they could give, to show them some of God's love – just as God did for us when he sent Jesus?

You could finish the time of quiet by listening to a CD that has a Christmas carol about God's gift of Jesus at Christmas (for example, 'O Little Town of Bethlehem', 'The First Nowell' or 'We Three Kings'). Alternatively, you could read the words of the carol out loud.

Wish everyone a very happy Christmas!

*Note:* If you don't wish to involve volunteers or it's not easy to do so, simply use the outline as above, omitting the sections about inviting volunteers to the front and giving instructions to them as you talk about the party. You can still set the scene by putting on the hat and badge yourself, playing the CD, and so on.

For other Christmas ideas for assemblies visit: **www.sloughbaptistchurch.org.uk/ schoolsweek**
You will need to pay £5 to download the material.

Christian groups in schools are also another forum for reaching out to young people with the good news of Christmas.

For resources for Christian groups in secondary schools go to **www.scriptureunion.org.uk/re-source** Click under 'meeting outlines' then 'archive' for downloads of Christmas outlines produced over the past few years.

For interesting facts about some of the customs of Christmas visit: **www.whychristmas.com**

For statistics, surveys and quotations try: **www.eauk.org/resources/info/statistics/ christmasstats2006.cfm**

# Challenging child

*An all-age nativity service based on Luke 1:26–38; 2:1–20; Matthew 1:18–24; 2:1–12*

## You will need

- simple costumes (for Mary, an angel, Joseph, shepherds, wise men) and props for the nativity scene (a large blue sheet or tablecloth, a large white sheet or tablecloth, a stool, a manger, hay or straw, a baby doll)

- three large gifts for the wise men – large enough to be visible to the congregation when placed in the tableau (different shaped boxes, wrapped in coloured, shiny paper, labelled: 'Gold', 'Frankincense', and 'Myrrh')
- gift-wrapping materials (wrapping paper, sticky tape, scissors)
- fun-sized chocolate bars to be wrapped, enough for everyone
- volunteers: for the nativity scene, to greet people, to provide drinks and mince pies, four readers
- service outlines for each tableau participant
- recording of Christmas music or musicians rehearsed and ready to play Christmas music

## Preparation

### The nativity tableau

The nativity tableau forms gradually throughout the service. The aim is to achieve a peaceful, reflective mood. Ask adults or older children to take part – to represent Mary, an angel, Joseph, three or four shepherds, and three wise men.

Explain to the volunteers that they will need to move into place during the hymns, then stay as still as possible – aiming to create a living picture of the nativity scene. Choose people who will be able to do this with dignity.

Supply the simple costumes and props that are appropriate for each character's role.

Decide everyone's position in advance and rehearse. Provide service outlines so that the participants can see when it's time for them to join in the scene.

## The scene

Set up one area, visible to the seated congregation, as the scene for the tableau – possibly elevated. Place a stool near the manger. Drape it with a large blue sheet or tablecloth. Just behind and to one side of this, spread, as if dropped, a large white sheet or tablecloth. Fill the manger with hay or straw and spread some on the floor.

Use simple lighting to focus on the nativity scene. Dim the main lights and have free-standing lamps or fairy lights around the nativity scene.

Set up a number of gift-wrapping 'stations' around the meeting area, with Christmas gift-wrap, sticky tape, scissors and little 'gifts' (fun-sized chocolate bars – one for each person attending the service).

As people gather they should be aware of the empty nativity scene so that this acts as the focus for the coming service. You could also display an image of the nativity scene on PowerPoint at the beginning and end of the service.

# Introductory activity

Have some Christmas music playing quietly.

Ask volunteers to greet the congregation and encourage them to wrap up a Christmas 'gift' at any of the gift-wrapping 'stations'. Encourage older and younger people to work together. Everyone should keep the 'gift' that they've wrapped with them during the service.

# Welcome and introduction

Welcome everyone to this service in which you'll be celebrating together an old, familiar story about a very special child.

Ask: 'How many children have taken part in nativity plays this Christmas? How many nativity plays have the adults been involved with or seen in their lifetimes?' Do a quick calculation to find the total number!

Explain that, as you all know the story so well, you are going to sing, see, tell and hear it all together now.

Say that you hope everyone has their wrapped present with them – they'll need these later in the service (leave some spare ones at the door for any latecomers).

# The story

**Sing:** 'Once in royal David's city'

**Tableau:** During the singing of verse 1, 'Mary' moves to her place, picks up and wraps the blue sheet around her as a cloak, then sits by the manger. The 'angel' gets into position, standing nearby, wrapping the white sheet over his shoulders.

After the hymn, lower the main lights, leaving on the lights focused on the nativity scene.

**Reader 1:** Luke 1:26–38

# A child is born

Ask the children what happens next. Fill in the story to the point where Mary and Joseph are in Bethlehem, there is no room for them in the inn and Jesus is born.

**Sing:** 'Away in a manger'

**Tableau:** During the hymn 'Joseph' joins the tableau and places the 'baby' in the manger by 'Mary'. 'Joseph' stands by 'Mary', together focusing on the 'baby'.

**Reader 2:** Luke 2:1–7

# Good news!

**Reader 3:** Luke 2:8–20

**Sing:** 'While shepherds watched their flocks by night'

**Tableau:** During the hymn, the 'shepherds' move into their places in the tableau.

# A very special baby

Comment on the shepherds' arrival. Ask the children about the nativity story. What gifts might the shepherds have brought for the baby? Who is missing from the nativity scene? The wise men, of course! Explain that it was probably some time after Jesus was born that these eastern visitors followed the star and found Jesus.

**Sing:** 'In the bleak midwinter'

**Tableau:** During the hymn, the 'wise men' bring their gifts, placing them so that they are visible to the audience, and join the scene.

**Reader 4:** Matthew 2:1–12

# Talk: A challenging child

Ask the children what gifts they might give a new baby today. Say that Jesus was no ordinary baby. He was special, so the wise men brought special gifts. Invite everyone to consider the gifts. Say: 'Let's see what the wise men brought the baby Jesus…'

Invite a child to pick up one of the three gifts from the tableau. Ask them to read the label aloud. Ask what this was and why it might have been given to Jesus. Talk about the gift, what it was and its significance.

Repeat this, with a different volunteer for each gift, talking about each one afterwards.

Say that the three gifts all pointed to the fact that Jesus was special and each one tells us something about who he is and what he would do.

- **Gold:** Jesus is a king, a ruler, Lord.

- **Frankincense:** it was used by priests in their worship to God. This showed that Jesus is a priest who came to help us know God. Incense also speaks of the holiness of God.

- **Myrrh:** it was used in the burial customs of the time and pointed to the death of Jesus.

Say that whilst we enjoy hearing the familiar Christmas story, it's not just a warm, comfortable story. Jesus was no ordinary child, but God's Son, Lord and King. Talk about the challenges the story of his birth brings:

- **Gold:** will we let God's Son, Jesus, rule in our lives?

- **Frankincense:** Jesus – a priest – came to help us know God. How well do we know him?

- **Myrrh:** Jesus gave his life for me. Have I said thank you to him for coming and dying for me?

Jesus' birth in the 'stable': Is there a place in our own lives for God's Son, Jesus, today?

Conclude by saying that Jesus' coming into our world is 'good news ... which will make everyone happy' (Luke 2:10). Whatever our situations this Christmas-time, God wants us to receive his comfort and joy – as we recognise him as King, Priest and Saviour.

## Time of quiet

In a short time of quiet ask everyone to think about what Jesus (King, Priest and Saviour) means to them. Invite everyone to hold the gift they wrapped earlier, whilst thinking about how the story of Jesus' birth challenges them. Encourage everyone to take this opportunity to thank God for giving his Son, or to decide to let him rule in their lives from now on. Whatever they'd like to say to God, ask them to imagine their 'gift' representing this.

## Conclusion

Invite everyone to worship Jesus as Lord and King now as you sing the final hymn together. If they'd like, during the hymn, they can bring their 'gift' to the manger as a sign of their own worship of Jesus. Help people place their 'gifts' near the manger in the tableau.

**Sing:** 'O come, all ye faithful'

## Prayer

Either lead the congregation in the following prayer or, if using PowerPoint or OHT, display the prayer and encourage everyone to say it together:

Lord Jesus, our King,
Thank you for coming into our world.
Help us to let you rule in our lives.
Lord Jesus, our Priest,
Thank you for coming so that we can know God.
Help us to draw near to you.
Lord Jesus, our Saviour,
Thank you for dying on the cross so that our sins can be forgiven.
Help us to accept and share your forgiveness now.
Lord God, thank you for the good news of Christmas.
May your joy and comfort fill our lives today and always.
Amen.

Thank everyone for coming and taking part in telling the story of the birth of Jesus – this special, challenging child. Invite everyone to stay for coffee or soft drinks and mince pies. Ask for a few volunteers (children or teenagers) to help you with something now.

Keep the tableau in place until the congregation moves around. Ask your volunteers to gather up the 'gifts' (from the tableau) and then distribute them to the congregation during coffee.

# A make-and-tell nativity

*An all-age service for Christmas based on Luke 2:8–20, by Peter Graystone*

## Concept

This is an extremely active service to which everyone in the congregation, from the youngest to the oldest, can contribute. During the service a model of the hills outside Bethlehem is created out of simple craft materials. It requires no rehearsal and no one needs to act or learn lines, but because it is participatory and involves movement, some thought must be given in advance to the practicalities.

## You will need

- live music or music on CD to play while the congregation are making things.
- model shelter about 20 cm high with Mary, Joseph and Jesus in a manger. Ideally this should be homemade from cardboard, straw and chenille wires. This could be bought or, with sufficient warning, a group of children from the church could be asked to make it.
- a low table placed at the front of the church with a large green sheet spread over it. Place the model of the manger scene in the corner. Put cushions or boxes under the sheet to give the impression of rolling hills surrounding the model. Behind the model, attach black paper to represent the night sky.
- white and black chenille wires, cotton wool balls, aluminium foil and Blu-tack. To work out the quantities required, round up the number of people you expect to the nearest fifty. For every fifty you will require 200 chenille wires (ideally 100 black and 100 white), fifty cotton wool balls (usually sold in packs of 100), 4 m aluminium foil (sold in various lengths, but 30 cm wide), and half a pack of Blu-tack. The cost of this will be about 15 pence per person.
- an atmospheric lighting for the end of the service (optional).

The craft materials should be arranged in advance of the service so that at the end of each row or pew there is a plastic freezer bag containing enough chenille wires, cotton wool, 15 cm squares of foil and Blu-tack for the people who will sit there.

## Welcome

The service leader should greet the congregation, introduce the model of the hillside surrounding Bethlehem, and ask them to echo each line of this opening prayer:

Lord Jesus born in Bethlehem,
Welcome to our world this Christmas,
Welcome to our church this Christmas,
Welcome in our homes this Christmas,
Welcome in our lives this Christmas,
Lord Jesus Christ, we praise you.

## Song

Begin with a well known and appropriate hymn such as 'O come, all you faithful'.

## Bible reading

Luke 2:8–20.

## Song

Choose a hymn which speaks of the birth of Jesus, such as 'Once in royal David's city'.

## Talk and demonstration

In two minutes of well-chosen words, refer back to the Bible reading about the shepherds being told of the birth of Jesus. Here, God (Jesus) comes in the form of a crying, feeding and helpless human being. If you knew that the most important person in history was born, who would you tell? Parliament? The newspapers? The BBC? God chose to tell... riff-raff! The shepherds on the hill were among the poorest people in Bethlehem, and they had a reputation for being rogues. I wonder why God chose to make himself known to such lowly people!

Explain that everyone is going to make a model of a shepherd to be part of the model of God born on earth. Demonstrate how to do this. Put a twist in one of the chenille wires to represent a head and arms (white or black – their choice). Thread another chenille wire through the head, and twist it so that it forms a body and legs. To help the shepherd stand up, make him a pair of shoes out of Blu-tack.

## Making and listening

The music group sings a Christmas song, or some pre-recorded music is played. While this is happening, everyone in the congregation makes a shepherd.

## Song

Choose a hymn which focuses on the shepherds, such as 'While shepherds watched their flocks by night'. As you announce it, invite the children to collect the shepherds from the people around them and bring them to the front of the church. (Suggest that the young ones bring a parent with them.) They give them to the people who are creating the model and return to their seats. The model makers arrange them on the hillside.

## Talk and demonstration

In another short talk explain more about the significance of Jesus' birth, overlooked by a field of sheep. Looking after sheep was the most ordinary job in the world. Perhaps God chose shepherds because he wanted to make it clear that he is important to every ordinary person in the world, no matter how poor or bad they are.

Show everyone how to make a sheep. This is slightly more complicated! Pull a cotton wool ball until there is a small hole in the middle of it. Take two Chenille wires (black ones give the best effect) and make two twists approximately one-third away from each end. The wire ends will form the front and back legs. Make a loop in the central third to form the head and twist to secure. Push the back legs through the middle of the cotton wool ball.

## Making and listening

Another song is performed or played. Everyone in the congregation makes a sheep.

## Song

Choose a hymn which mentions flocks of sheep or shepherds, such as 'God rest you merry gentlemen', or 'Come and join the celebration'. Ask the children to collect the sheep which have been made and bring them to the front to be added to the model, as before.

## Talk and demonstration

The third two-minute talk is about stars. Say that they must have gone dim with the brightness of the angels, but one of them was significant because it showed the place where Jesus had been born. The message of the angels was that God is glorious, peace is possible, and that humans can find God to be a Saviour.

Make a star by crumpling and shaping a piece of aluminium foil. (There is no particular instruction for the congregation to obey here - just squeeze!) Put a generous piece of Blu-tack in the middle so that it can be attached to the black paper.

## Making and listening

There is more music, during which everyone in the congregation makes a star.

## Song

Sing a hymn which mentions stars, such as 'See amid the winter's snow', or 'It was on a starry night'. Stars are brought to the front as before, and helpers use the Blu-tack to stick

them to the 'sky' above the model. This time, however, suggest that the children stay at the front of the room and sit cross-legged on the floor in front of the model so that they can get a good view of it.

## Talk

Sum up briefly by rejoicing that God came to earth not just for shepherds on a hillside, but for you and me as well. The Bible tells us that the shepherds went away praising God and telling everyone they knew. How will you go away? Will you tell people that you have had a glimpse of Jesus this Christmas? If it is true, then it will make a permanent difference to your whole life!

## Song

Sing a hymn which will be well known to the children, such as 'Away in a manger'. To make the service truly memorable, try to create a moment of wonder at this point in the service. Depending on the nature of the building, it may be possible to sing by candlelight, or just dim the lights until only a spotlight remains on the model, or use a mirror ball to send dots of light dancing around the walls.

## Prayers

Invite the person who is leading intercessions to pray for:

• The events in the world's news, especially for those celebrating Christmas from a context of poverty or hunger;
• The needs of particular people in the church, including those for whom Christmas this year is a time of sadness;
• Safety for those who are travelling or working this Christmas;
• Peace and justice for those who live in the land where Jesus was born.

## Song

Close with a rousing hymn such as 'Hark the herald angels sing', or 'See him lying on a bed of straw', during which the children can return to their places.

## Blessing

Lord Jesus Christ,
May the good things of Christmas stay with us
Every day of the coming week,
Every week of the coming year,
Every year of our lives,
Until we meet you face to face. Amen.

# Come to the light

*A service for all ages suitable for Christmas Day based on Luke 2:25–35*

## Preparation

Place a Christmas tree in a prominent place. Have a set of lights on it, but do not switch them on. Have Christmas ornaments ready to hang on it – ideally one for each of the lines of the 'Call to worship'. Alternatively, ask people to bring their own tree ornaments, but make sure you have a candle ornament and a star.

## For the talk

Have three contrasting photos of babies that can be shown to the congregation, for example, on OHP or PowerPoint. The first could be peaceful or smiling, the second crying and the third surprised (although this one is not essential). Ideally they should show adult members of the congregation when they were babies – including the speaker. Also have some comments made about the babies written up on OHT or PowerPoint. These will be revealed at the appropriate times as explained in the talk.

## Arrival

Create an expectant atmosphere for people to come in to – not too jolly and not too light – with suitable music playing. Give each person a candle as they come in. If you have been using an advent ring or crown, light all five candles at the start of the service.

## Call to worship

As the call to worship is said, invite people to hang the ornaments on the tree. The first should be a candle ornament, with a star for the last line.

We are called to celebrate the gift of God in Jesus Christ.
*For the 12 days of Christmas and for ever.*

Like the angel on the hillside we announce that Jesus is born.
*For the 12 days of Christmas and for ever.*

Like the multitude of angels we praise God with great joy.
*For the 12 days of Christmas and for ever.*

Like the shepherds we gather eagerly around the baby.
*For the 12 days of Christmas and for ever.*

Like the people of Bethlehem we hear what God has done.
*For the 12 days of Christmas and for ever.*

Like Joseph we obey what God has spoken.
*For the 12 days of Christmas and for ever.*

Like Mary we ponder the wonder of God acting through us.
*For the 12 days of Christmas and for ever.*

Like the manger we cradle the light God has given.
*For the 12 days of Christmas and for ever.*

Like the stars we shine with the brilliance of good news.
*For the 12 days of Christmas and for ever.*

Like Simeon we look forward to seeing the Saviour.
*For the 12 days of Christmas and for ever.*

Like Anna we tell others what we know.
*For the 12 days of Christmas and for ever.*

Once the tree is decorated, turn on the lights.

## Welcome

Welcome everyone to this Christmas morning service, in which we remember that Jesus was born to be a light to all people. You could use the following introduction, which refers to the candles on an advent ring or crown:

The time of Advent waiting is over! Today we celebrate the birth of Jesus. The Advent candles of hope, peace, joy and love are lit. The final candle is lit, reminding us that God has done what he promised – Jesus has been born. The lights are lit on the Christmas tree, a reminder that Jesus is the light that shines for ever for all people.

## Song

'Come and join the celebration'

## Bible reading

Luke 2:25–35

This can be read by a narrator with an older man speaking Simeon's words. 'Simeon' could sing verses 29 to 32 (for example, as in the song 'Faithful Vigil Ended'). Alternatively, actors could perform as Joseph, Mary and Simeon, with Simeon learning his part beforehand.

## Song

'Joy to the world'

## Story

Show a variety of candles and gradually light them as you talk. Point out some of the differences – size, shape, smell, the amount of light they give – or ask the congregation to do so. Ask what the candles are used for – birthdays, to create a romantic atmosphere, in a power cut, at parties. One candle on its own is not very bright, but together they can give a lot of light. We are all called to shine together with the light of the good news of Jesus. You could tell the following story:

Years ago, before electricity was available, people used candles as their main source of light. Two boys, Hans and Karl, lived high up in the Alps in Switzerland, where there was a white Christmas every year. They were great friends and always walked to school together. Their school was several miles away and in the winter it was always dark when they set out to school and dark by the time they got home. So as well as their books, they each carried a candle to school. The candles that the children took with them were the only lights in the school. When the children arrived, they would shake the snow off their boots at the door and then place their candles safely in the candle holders on their desks. By the time all the children had arrived the whole room would be a blaze of light. The teacher didn't have any trouble calling the register in the winter as he could see immediately if someone was missing – no candle, no child!

One day, as Hans and Karl were walking to school they had a quarrel. It was only a silly quarrel, but Hans decided he didn't want to walk with Karl and took the short cut over the frozen river, even though he knew that it was dangerous. Karl went on alone and arrived at school. He sat down at his desk and lit his candle. There was no light at the desk next to him. There was no sign of Hans. Without saying anything, Karl got up, put his boots and heavy coat back on and trudged back up the path to where the two boys had parted company earlier. It was now light and Karl could see Hans' footprints in the snow, so he followed them. He crossed the frozen river and there was still no sign of Hans. Eventually the footprints stopped and there was Hans asleep in the snow, still clutching his candle. He had got lost and fallen asleep from tiredness and the snow was beginning to drift over him. But Karl swept the snow away with his hands and gave Hans a piggyback to school.

Soon the boys were back at their desks, warmed up, candles alight and hard at work. The light given by Karl and Hans' candles in that old schoolroom wasn't very great, but with the light of the other boys' candles the lights together made a great impact.

## Song

'The light of Christ' or 'In the bleak midwinter'

## All-age talk

*(See the preparation section at the beginning of this service material.)*

**A beautiful baby:** Show your first baby photo. Ask the congregation: if you were seeing this baby for the first time, what might you say? Go round and get some answers from people of different ages. Reveal the first set of written-up comments which need to be typical positive comments for such occasions: 'Aah! She's beautiful!' 'What a lovely baby!' 'He's got his father's eyes.' 'What a lot of hair!' 'That's a fine pair of lungs!'

Talk about the arrival of Mary and Joseph with the baby Jesus in the Temple (Luke 2:22–24). Introduce the character of Simeon – a man who loved God and was longing for God to do something to rescue his people. When he saw the baby Jesus at the Temple, what would we expect him to say? Refer back to your list, then to verses 28 to 32.

- Jesus was indeed a beautiful sight for Simeon – he recognised that Jesus was the one God had sent to save his people. At last!
- Simeon talked about what Jesus was like, not his hair or nose, but calling him a light. Jesus would reveal God to the world. Refer to your lights and candles from earlier in the service.

**A tough future:** Show your second baby photo to the congregation and again get their comments. Reveal the second set of less positive, baby comments: 'He looks just like Winston Churchill.' 'Does she always cry like that?' 'She looks just like ET.' 'You've got a tough job ahead of you.'

Talk about the things Simeon went on to say about Jesus (verses 34 and 35):

- Some people would be against Jesus.
- Mary would know great sadness because of him.

We know how both of those things were seen most clearly when Jesus died on the cross. That was God's plan for this baby – a tough future, but one that would save people from being separated from God.

**The big choice**: Show the third baby photo and listen to their comments. Reveal your final baby comment: 'All babies look the same to me.' Point out that not everyone wants to 'Ooh!' and 'Aah!' over babies. You might just want to shrug your shoulders and that's fair enough. But the baby Jesus is different. Simeon knew that Jesus would split people into two groups – those who loved him and those who were against him. Loving him isn't just about liking the idea of a sweet baby, but of seeing all that he went on to do – wanting to have all that is dark in our lives swept away by his wonderful light. Then Jesus will be wonderful, joyful news for us, too – the best ever.

## Song

Sing one of the following:

'O little town of Bethlehem'
'Silent night'
'Born in the night'
'Mary's child'
'Go, tell it on the mountain'
'Infant Holy'

## Prayer

Ask a few people to prepare some topics for intercession beforehand, or ask the congregation for suggestions. At the end of each topic, finish with the response:

'Lord Jesus, you are the light,
*Shine in the darkness.*'

You might end as follows, saying:

'When Jesus was born, God gave the world his best gift.
Help us Lord, to give each other your light this Christmas. Amen.'

## Song

'Hark the herald angel sing'

## Prayer

Light each person's candle – perhaps from the central candle on an advent ring or crown. When all the candles are lit, the following may be said:

O God, giver of light to the world,
*May your light shine brightly in us today.*
Thank you for all your gifts to us,
*May your light shine brightly in us today.*
As we celebrate the birth of Jesus,
*May your light shine brightly in us today.*

Suggest that you each take your candle home and give it to someone who has not been to church today as an act of sharing God's light.

## Closing prayer

'God of hope and peace and joy and love, come and walk with us.
Through our lives and our words, spread your light in the world. Amen.'

*An interactive service for all ages based on Luke 2:1–20, celebrating that God has given us his Son*

## Preparation

Prepare six boxes (for example, shoeboxes) wrapped in Christmas paper with one of the following words or phrases on each box 'peace', 'joy', 'for everyone', 'good news', 'Saviour', 'Christ the Lord'. To each box attach a length of string that will stretch from the front out into the congregation.

Gather together sufficient materials to dress up six volunteers as 'instant' angels, for example, white sheets, white dresses, net curtains, pieces of tinsel.

Make five large cards with one of the following words on each: 'angel', 'sing', 'noisy', 'manger', 'now'.

Each member of the congregation will need a sheet of A5 pastel coloured paper, cut into the shape of a paper angel, a paper clip and pens or pencils. Place the materials in a plastic bag or wallet for each group of ten people, and distribute the 'kits' around the building or to stewards in advance, ready to be used when needed during the service.

Provide the words and music of all the songs, including either the live soloist, or the recorded version of 'What kind of greatness' (*Rumours of angels* by Graham Kendrick, Make Way Music, 1994).

## Song

'Angels from the realms of glory'

## Introductory activity

Ask people to form groups of two or three and share together what they did to celebrate a recent birthday. Make sure all ages take part. After a few minutes invite volunteers to share with the whole congregation some of the ways in which they celebrated. Close by saying that today we are celebrating a very special birthday: the day the Son of God was born.

## Reading

Invite two members of the congregation to read Luke 2:1–7,8–20.

## Song

'O little town of Bethlehem'

## Story

Tell the following story and encourage the congregation to respond to the key words with the actions or phrases as appropriate every time they are used. Ask volunteers to hold up each of the key words. You will need to teach these as you go through the story, with plenty of repetition. Elaborate on the story below if you wish.

Imagine you are in heaven. There is a large group of angels getting ready for a great big celebration. In fact the greatest, biggest celebration that has ever happened in the whole history of the world! *(Ask a volunteer to hold up the 'angel' card. Encourage everyone to raise their hands and say 'Glory to God' whenever they hear this word.)*

The angels had to learn to fly in formation and then to practise a new song to sing.

*(Ask a volunteer to hold up the 'sing' card. Encourage everyone to sing 'Hallelujah' (to the tune of the opening word of the 'Hallelujah Chorus' from* The Messiah*) whenever they hear this word.)*

Gabriel was the chief angel and he made sure they were all in tune and knew the words. All the angels were very well behaved as they learned to sing, except one. This angel was not really naughty, not really rebellious, but he was rather noisy. *(Ask a volunteer to hold up the 'noisy' card. Encourage everyone to wave and say 'Hello, Mum. It's me!' whenever they hear this word.)*

Whatever the angels were doing, 'Noisy' was always there as well, making a disturbance because he was so excited. The important thing that the angels had to practise, was knowing when they had to begin this great celebration! Gabriel told them that they had to wait until they heard him say the word 'manger'. *(Ask a volunteer to hold up the 'manger' card. Encourage everyone to say 'It's time to go!' whenever they hear this word.)*

This was rather difficult to get right. They had to learn to fly, and to sing, and to go but only when they heard the word 'manger'. Of course, every time they practised this, 'Noisy' kept on getting it wrong. Eventually, the great day arrived; actually it was not a day, but a night. All the angels in heaven watched Gabriel fly down to earth. He had to get the attention of the shepherds on the hillside. I think he rather overdid it. There was a brilliant light as he appeared, and those poor men were absolutely terrified. Gabriel had a great speech worked

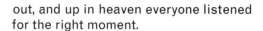

out, and up in heaven everyone listened for the right moment.

'Don't be afraid,' Gabriel said.

Noisy asked, 'Now?' (*Ask a volunteer to hold up the 'now' card. Encourage everyone to respond 'No' whenever they hear this word.*)

'Good news of great joy,' Gabriel said.

Noisy asked, 'Now?'

'Today in the town of David' ... 'Now?'

'A baby wrapped in cloth' ... 'Now?'

'Lying in a manger.' (*Wait for the response, 'It's time to go!'*)

The angels began to sing and sing and sing... (*At this point ask the musicians to play 'O come, let us adore him' and then all join in singing this chorus through twice.*)

So then the angels left and flew back to heaven in backwards formation, except for one. 'Noisy' swooped over the shepherds and followed them down the hill into Bethlehem. When they went into a stable, he ducked in behind them and gasped at what he saw.

He went very quiet and said, 'Ah, now is the time to worship.'

## Song

'Come now is the time to worship'

## Creative activity

For this activity you will need a person dressed as an angel who is located near the front of the worship area higher than everyone else (for example, in a pulpit or on a platform). He or she should hold tightly the six loose ends of the string attached to the six boxes nearby. The leader explains that at the heart of the celebration of Christmas is Jesus, God's gift to us. The boxes show the gifts God promised us through the words of the angels.

Invite some children to help. (Give each child a few items to dress themselves in, making 'instant angel' outfits.) Ask the 'angels' to take the boxes out into the congregation one at a time and give them out. It would be most effective if the strings were of varying lengths to stretch out into different parts of the congregation. As this is happening the leader comments on the gifts that God has given to us through the coming of Jesus, using the words shown on the gift boxes. Explain that the good news of Christmas is that God's own Son,

Christ the Lord, has come to live amongst us to be our Saviour. Because Jesus has come we can know and experience joy and peace with God. This good news is for everyone.

(*Be careful about the boxes and strings stretched around the church, that it does not become a hazard. If you can tie the loose end of the strings onto something, you may like to leave them in place until the end of the service.*)

Distribute the paper angel templates, paper clips and pens or pencils. Demonstrate how to make an angel by folding the plain paper lengthways in two, and tearing the shape whilst folded. (The torn edges give added texture.) Open the paper out and then invite each person to think of which of God's 'Christmas gifts' people in the world most need to hear about today, then write or draw something on their angel shape to show this. (For example, for 'peace', they might draw weapons or write 'end fighting'; for 'joy', they might write the name of someone they know who is sad and needs to know God's love.) Offer help to children, as needed. Invite each person to attach their paper angel to one of the strings stretching down from the central angel to the gift boxes. Whilst people are doing this, use the song 'What kind of greatness' either sung as a solo or played from the CD (from *Rumours of Angels* by Graham Kendrick, Make Way Music 1994). The congregation could join in the chorus towards the end of the song.

## Prayer

Invite three prepared people to lead everyone in prayer. You could invite the congregation to say together the angels 'song' in between each section. Use the version of Luke 2:14 from the Good News Bible for this response: 'Glory to God in the highest heaven and peace on earth to those with whom he is pleased.'

## Song

'O come, all ye faithful'

# Christmas journeys

*An all-age service based on Matthew 1:18–21; Luke 2:1–14 to celebrate that God himself made a journey that first Christmas, from heaven to earth to save us*

## Preparation

Collect together a bicycle (use this as far as it is appropriate for your church and its building) and baby equipment that will be too awkward to carry on a bike – such as a bath, a chair, a bag of nappies, a blanket, a duvet, a cuddly toy.

You will also need a hula-hoop and six tinsel-covered sticks the same length as the diameter of the hoop. These will be laid across and tied on to either side of the hoop during the game, like the spokes of a wheel. Practice this beforehand. (Lay three sticks under and three on top of the hoop.) Attach to each spoke a luggage label on which one of the questions for the game is written. Before the service, hide the six spokes in the building where they can easily be spotted.

Find a shepherd's costume and circles of paper and pencils.

Make sure that the song words appear on PowerPoint, on acetate or the service sheet.

## Introduction

How did people travel to the service? Conduct a poll, putting the results on an overhead projector, or devise a bar chart. Cars and walking are the most likely; there may be some cyclists, buggies, motorbikes; boats and planes are possibilities in some places! Introduce the idea of journeys.

## Song

'See him lying on a bed of straw' or 'Oh little town of Bethlehem'

## Game and Bible reading

Invite younger children to find the six hidden spokes. Once all six have been found, explain that there is a question on each. (You will need to adjust the exact words of the questions according to the version of the Bible that you are using.)

1 Who was Mary engaged to?
2 What was Joseph doing when the angel spoke to him?
3 What was the baby to be called and what did the name mean?
4 What was the name of the emperor who called for the census?
5 Where did Joseph have to go to register?
6 What was Bethlehem famous for?

The child with question one reads out their question, perhaps helped by an older child. Then read Matthew 1:18–21 followed by Luke 2:1–4. As the children hear the answer to the question, they put up their hands. (Once you have the correct answer, tie the spoke in place on the hoop and the second child reads out their question, and so on.)

## Talk

So Mary and Joseph had to go to Bethlehem. Imagine it was today. Mary was expecting a baby soon. What would she take with her? Show all the equipment you have collected. She may have walked. She may have gone on a donkey. Let's imagine though that she went on a bicycle, which may be the nearest most of us would get to a donkey! How much do you think she could manage to carry? Invite a volunteer to be loaded up with the equipment as they sit astride a bike. It will be impossible and funny! Mary in fact probably took very little with her, hoping, no doubt, that a friendly family would come to help her. Anyway, babies didn't have much equipment then, certainly not disposable nappies, or a baby bath! Briefly fill in the story up to the point where Jesus is born.

Mary and Joseph went on a long journey. But it was all the more extraordinary that God himself came from heaven to earth. He came to live as a human being just like you and me! This journey is hard for us to begin to understand. Baby Jesus was God, who had become human! Why did he come? – To save his people from their sins.

## Song

'From heaven you came, helpless babe'

## Prayers

If you have time beforehand with a group of children, ask them to create a prayer like the one below, which is made up of thanking, confessing and asking God. (It was devised by a group of 8- to 10-year old children for Christmas 2003.) Otherwise ask a group of children to pray this prayer.

**All together:** Dear God…
**Child 1:** Thank you for Christmas presents.
**Child 2:** Thank you for the birth of Jesus.
**Child 3:** Thank you for cards and food and the decorations on the tree.
**Child 4:** Thank you for a time to be with our families.

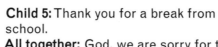

**Child 5:** Thank you for a break from school.

**All together:** God, we are sorry for the wrong things we have done.
*(Pause.)*

**All together:** We are sad about the war that happened this year. *(Adapt as necessary.)*

**Child 1:** Please help the world to be a better place.

**Child 2:** Please help us to have fun at Christmas.

**Child 3:** Please help the homeless at Christmas.

**Child 4:** Please help us get on with our brothers and sisters.

**Child 5:** Please help us remember that Jesus came at Christmas to save us from our sins.

**All together:** Happy Birthday, Jesus! Amen.

## Shepherd's interview

Someone dressed as a shepherd, cycles into church screeching to a halt next to the interviewer. (Adapt this script to suit you.)

**Interviewer:** Hey, you nearly knocked me over!

**Shepherd:** Sorry, but I'm in a rush. Can't stop!

**Interviewer:** But who are you? And why are you dressed in a dressing gown with a tea towel around your head?

**Shepherd:** That's what shepherds wore in the Middle East 2,000 years ago. Sunblock and baseball caps had not yet been invented! It's to keep the sun off our heads, and to keep us warm as we look after our sheep in the cold night-time.

**Interviewer:** And had bicycles been invented?

**Shepherd:** No, neither cars nor submarines nor... but I was in such a hurry that when I saw this bike, I jumped on it... It's faster than a donkey! Now, I must go. I've got to tell my wife what I've just seen.

**Interviewer:** What have you seen?

**Shepherd:** Well, we shepherds were sitting with the sheep throughout the night, making sure no wolves got hold of our sheep. It was pretty dark out when suddenly the sun shot over the horizon. At least that's what I thought it was. The sky was filled with very bright light and the ground shook with loud music, just like a rock concert, except I'm not meant to know about rock concerts!

**Interviewer:** What was it?

**Shepherd:** Messengers from God – angels. They sang so loudly and they told us that a baby had just been born in the village at the bottom of the hill. This baby had come from God. He was going to rescue people. And we were to go and see him!

**Interviewer:** What did you do then?

**Shepherd:** We jumped to our feet, rushed down the hill, straight to where we could hear a tiny baby crying. He was lying in a hay box; his mum

and dad were gazing at him, looking sort of shocked. And his mum looked pretty tired, too. We all talked at once, wanting to know his name, where he came from, did they have everything they needed, could my wife help, that sort of thing. Then we told them what had happened to us and then came away.

**Interviewer:** Did he look like an ordinary baby?

**Shepherd:** Oh yes, red in the face and scrunched up like new babies usually look. Very ordinary.

**Interviewer:** Can I ask you...

**Shepherd:** No, I can't stay any longer. Now, how do you ride a bicycle? *(He falls off once and then cycles away.)*

## Song

'While shepherds watched'

## Prayer

Invite everyone to stand up and get into circles of eight. Give each person a circular sheet of paper and pencil to write or draw what aspect of Christmas they want to thank God for. One person in each circle collects all the circles of paper.

Read each of the following prayers and, after each, sing the chorus of 'Oh come, all ye faithful'. You could invite people to hold hands to make a better wheel.

**Leader:** We thank you, God, that Mary and Joseph obeyed you and were willing to be the parents of your Son, Jesus, even though life was sometimes very hard, but other times full of joy. Thank you that they made the journey to Bethlehem.

**All sing:** *Oh come, let us adore him...*

**Leader:** We thank you, God, that the first people who heard about Jesus were ordinary people – shepherds – who came to worship you. Thank you that they were willing to make the journey to see the newborn baby Jesus.

**All sing:** *Oh come, let us adore him...*

**Leader:** We thank you, God, that you were willing to make the journey to come to this earth. We thank you that Jesus lived up to his name – he came to save his people from their sins.

**All sing:** *Oh come, let us adore him...*

**Leader:** Thank you, God, for all the joy of Christmas. Thank you especially for... *(Ask the person in each circle holding the circles of paper to call out what has been written or drawn on the circles.)*

**All sing:** *Oh come, let us adore him...*

## Song

Choose a final hymn known to everyone.

# Spelling out Christmas

*An all-age nativity service with readings from Isaiah and Luke, by Marjory Francis*

## You will need

- nine cards (at least A3 size) with the letters C H R I S T M A S on them
- headgear for the children: tinsel rings (angels), cloth squares and stretch bands made from knotted tights (shepherds) and simple crowns (wise men)
- Mary, Joseph, Simeon and Isaiah in costume; a 'baby'; a scroll for Isaiah
- someone to carry a star
- two narrators and one reader
- row of nine chairs at the front of the church

## Preparation

Make the letters bold enough to be seen by everybody. They could be painted or collaged as part of an earlier activity. The letters spelling 'CHRIST' should be in one colour (for example, red) and 'MAS' in another (for example, green). (Alternatively, if you have suitable technology, you could display the letters in colour on a screen.)

Distribute the letters around the building, each one near enough to a seat for someone to feel it is their responsibility to take it to the front at the appropriate time. (Not delegating these in advance adds to the spontaneity of the service and people's involvement.)

The reader should read from a Bible.

## On the way in

Ask each child to choose an item of headgear: tinsel if they would like to be an angel, a cloth and stretch band for a shepherd, or a crown for a wise man. Say that they will be told when to wear it and what to do.

## Welcome and introduction

Warmly welcome everyone to the service. Say that today you will be spelling out together what Christmas is all about. Lots of people will be taking part, and there might be surprises for some!

**Narrator 1:** 'C' is for Creation. *(Invite the person nearest the letter 'C' to bring it and sit on the first chair. Make sure the letter is held on the person's lap for everyone to see.)*

**Narrator 1:** Yes, 'C' is for Creation.
**Narrator 2:** God made a beautiful world.
**Narrator 1:** There were mountains and fountains...

**Narrator 2:** trees and bees ...
**Narrator 1:** dogs and frogs...
**Narrator 2:** and seven seas...
**Narrator 1:** or even more. Turn to your neighbour and say one amazing thing that God has made.
**Narrator 2:** Let's thank God for his beautiful world.

## Song

'All things bright and beautiful'

**Narrator 1:** 'H' is for Heaven. *(Invite the person nearest the 'H' to bring it and sit on the next chair.)*

**Narrator 2:** Imagine the angels in heaven looking down on God's world.
**Narrator 1:** They would see that it was beautiful...
**Narrator 2:** and that it was 'fruit-i-ful'...
**Narrator 1:** but that people were not dutiful.
**Narrator 2:** Yes, everything had gone wrong.
**Narrator 1:** People had spoilt God's world. They were fighting...
**Narrator 2:** and backbiting...
**Narrator 1:** and grabbing...
**Narrator 2:** and stabbing.
**Narrator 1:** It was horrible to see...
**Narrator 2:** and was all caused by you and me.
**Narrator 1:** Pause and think about how you have helped to spoil God's creation. Then please join in the response 'Father, forgive' after each phrase in the following prayer:

## Prayer

For the times when I have not been loving, *Father, forgive.*
For the times when I have not cared for others...
For the times when I have been selfish...
For the times when I have been unkind...
For the times when I have not been willing to share my possessions, my money, my time...
We thank you, Lord God that you have made it possible for us to be forgiven.

**Narrator 1:** So, how was God going to deal with the horrible things going on in his world? Well, 'R' is for Remedy and Rescue. *(Invite the person nearest 'R' to the front.)*

**Narrator 2:** God decided he would come and rescue his people. He would take on himself the punishment for all those wrong things.
**Narrator 1:** He sent prophets to tell people what he would do.

**Narrator 2:** One of them was this man. 'I' is for Isaiah. *(Invite the person nearest 'I' to the front. Isaiah also walks forward and hands his scroll to the reader.)*

# Reading

Isaiah 9:6; 53:4–6

# Song

'Come on and celebrate'

**Narrator 1:** 'S' is for Simeon. *(Invite the person nearest the red 'S' to the front. Simeon also comes forward.)*

**Narrator 2:** This is Simeon, a very old man. God had promised he would see the rescuer. He was waiting, and waiting, and waiting, until…

**Narrator 1:** 'T' is for Time. *(Invite the person nearest 'T' to the front.)*

**Narrator 2:** Yes, it was God's time. The stars in heaven were ready to proclaim God's coming. The Romans had built good roads for communication and had called for a census. Bethlehem was soon to become the centre of the universe.

**Narrator 1:** 'M' is for the Message to Mary. *(Invite the person nearest 'M' to the front. Mary also comes forward.)*

**Narrator 2:** God had a message for Mary.

# Reading

Luke 1:26–38

# Song

'Away in a manger'

*(During the song, Mary and Joseph arrange themselves with the baby.)*

**Narrator 1:** 'A' is for Angels. *(Invite the person nearest 'A' to the front.)*

**Narrator 2:** Angels told the shepherds the good news about Jesus' birth. As the angels and shepherds come forward, let's sing our next song.

# Song

'While shepherds watched'

*(Angels and shepherds arrange themselves near Mary and Joseph.)*

**Narrator 1:** 'S' is for Star. *(Invite the person nearest the green 'S' to the front.)*

**Narrator 2:** A star in the sky guided the wise men to Jesus. 'Wise men, please follow the star!'

# Song

'As with gladness'

*(The 'star' leads the 'wise men' to the front.)*

# Talk

Point out that we have spelled out 'Christmas' and we can see what stands out – 'Christ'. *(Indicate the first six red letters.)* Jesus Christ is at the centre of Christmas; it is all about him. *(Bring forward the people with the letters H I M.)* Jesus rightly should be the centre of our Christmas celebrations.

But there are others in the story, too. *(Let H I M sit down. Bring forward C A S T.)* There was a large cast of characters. Ask for suggestions as to who these might have been. Say that Mary and Joseph were in the centre of the story and had a very close relationship with Jesus. Simeon was very involved too. But there were others, like the poor shepherds and the rich wise men, who found themselves unexpectedly part of the cast and welcomed the involvement. There were many others around too, such as the people of Bethlehem and the Roman soldiers. Did they welcome their part in the story, or just ignore what was happening?

And because this is the story of God coming to live among us, we are part of the cast, too. Are we just going to have a walk on and walk off part and leave it all behind us once Christmas is over? *(Make MISS.)* Don't miss out!

*(Put the letters back in order.)*

Ask everyone to think quietly about Jesus Christ being at the centre of Christmas, and to make their own response to him. Finish with the following prayer:

'Lord Jesus, you are the Creator of our world. This Christmas, may we make you the centre of our lives and give you our worship. Amen.'

# Song

'O come, all ye faithful'

*Four ideas to enrich a family Christmas*

## Peace on earth

**You will need:** *a globe or map of the world, Post-it notes, pens*

Display a large map of the world where you can all see it. Read out the angels' message about peace on earth (Luke 2:14). Take a few minutes to think about a situation in the world that needs to know God's peace. Adults can help children in their thinking, as appropriate. Then write a short prayer for peace on a Post-it note and stick it on the map in the area you were thinking of.

## A family tree

**You will need:** *some large twigs placed either in a vase or firmly set in a pot with plaster (the twigs may be sprayed with silver or gold paint), enough luggage labels for all the members of your family you can think of, pens, family photographs (optional)*

Give everyone a label to personalise with their own name, their birthday and a drawing or photograph. Encourage them to make a similar label for each grandparent, cousin, aunt and uncle they have. Look at photographs of any older members of the family (such as great-grandparents) whom the children may never have known. Make a label for each of those people, too. Fasten all the labels onto the twigs as a family tree, and count them.

Thank God for each person who has been a part of your family.

As you think about all the people in perhaps three or four generations of your own family who are (or were) an important part of your history, remember how Jesus descended from King David (28 generations previously) and also other important people (such as Abraham) before him. You can read all their names in Matthew 1.

## Special presents

**You will need:** *oddments of card, wrapping paper, curling ribbon, paper, sticky tape and small empty boxes (for example, matchboxes or stock-cube boxes)*

Ask everyone to think about a special present that they were given for their birthday or a previous Christmas. Take it in turns to say why you liked it and, if possible, show it.

Read Matthew 2:1–12 together. What presents did the wise men give to Jesus? Why did they choose those gifts instead of the usual kinds of presents people give to babies?

Think about what gift you would choose to give Jesus, and why. If you would like to, write or draw it on a slip of paper and put it inside a small box to gift wrap later.

Make some present-shaped decorations from the assortment of craft materials, and hang them on your Christmas tree to remind you of the special presents given by the wise men to Jesus.

## Birth announcement

**You will need:** *national or local newspapers, paper, metallic and gel pens, a red or gold candle (or sealing wax) and matches, red or gold ribbon*

Look at the birth announcement columns in the newspapers. Read a few out aloud. Talk about the wording people have chosen to announce the birth of their child or grandchild.

Imagine how the birth of Jesus might have been publicly announced in the 'Bethlehem News', either by Mary and Joseph, or by God himself. Write a birth announcement for Jesus. Younger children can join in by doing a drawing, perhaps a smiley face.

Make the paper into a scroll by carefully melting a blob of wax and attaching a small piece of ribbon. Hang up your announcement.

# Short dramas

## Jesus is born

*Improvised drama for younger children*

**You will need:** *Bible, props such as a 'record' book (a scroll), a bag, a doll, baby clothes or cloth for the doll, some hay*

Put the children into three groups.

Tell today's story in three scenes (see below). After scene one is read out, encourage group one act it out; then group two will act out scene two and finally group three will dramatise scene three. Then repeat the story, but with different groups acting each scene; repeat the story a third time (this time reading it from Luke 2:1–7) so that each group has a chance to act out the whole story.

**Scene 1:** The Emperor Augustus gave orders for everyone to report to their home towns so that their names could be listed in the record books.

**Scene 2:** Joseph lived in a place called Nazareth in Galilee, but he was from the family of King David, and King David's home town was Bethlehem. So Joseph had to go to Bethlehem to have his name listed in the record books there. Joseph was engaged to a young woman called Mary, so she also had to go along with him to Bethlehem.

**Scene 3:** While Joseph and Mary were in Bethlehem, Mary gave birth to a baby boy – Jesus. Mary dressed her newborn baby in baby clothes. There was no room for them to stay in the inn, so Mary laid baby Jesus in a bed of hay.

## Wrapped up in chaos?

*Modern day improvised drama for two to three actors by Vicki Blyth*

**Characters:** *two neighbours who are quite eccentric with exaggerated accents*

Betty, a non-Christian, is busy preparing for Christmas in a very chaotic manner – trying to wrap presents and decorate a tree; it is evident she is unprepared!

Yvonne, a Christian, turns up for coffee – Betty doesn't put down her tools to talk with her friend. Instead she tries to have a conversation while she continues to prepare.

Yvonne opens the conversation by asking how Betty's preparation for Christmas is going. This part of the drama is best done ad-lib where possible as it will work better if it is shaped by the actors and how they interact.

As the conversation attempts to continue Betty is busy wrapping presents, clearly in a rush and the last present she has is a mug tree, with no box. Consequently the branches poke through the paper and she ends up re-wrapping it. Yvonne stops her and suggests calmly that it would be better to wrap it in the box. (The box should be clearly visible to the audience!) Betty sits and for the first time in the whole drama pauses for a moment and there is a realisation that yes, she's been so busy she hasn't really taken note of what she's doing.

The point here is that it is so easy to get caught up in the commercialism of Christmas that we forget why we celebrate. This point could be concluded with the actors or by a speaker who continues by taking the drama as a catalyst for his or her talk.

This can also be done with various 'freezes' taking place throughout, controlled by a professor-type character who freezes them using a sound and then makes a comment on what they're doing. For example, there can be a freeze when 'Yvonne' arrives and 'Betty' ignores her initially and the 'professor' could include a comment like: 'As you can see Betty is pre-occupied at the moment to even notice her friend Yvonne has arrived. Let's see what happens next.' Freezes should be limited to three in order for the dialogue to have fluidity.

## Shepherds

*A new look at the shepherds' story*

**Characters:** two narrators

**Narrator 1:** One night in the fields near Bethlehem some shepherds were guarding their sheep.

**Narrator 2:** A night in the fields with sheep. Ho hum. Boring. *(Yawns.)*

**Narrator 1:** Excuse me! *(Coughs and starts again.)* One night in the fields near Bethlehem some shepherds were guarding their sheep—

**Narrator 2:** I've heard that shepherds weren't the best-liked guys in town.

**Narrator 1:** *(Glaring at Narrator 1.)* Excuse me, I have an important narration to narrate! One night in the fields near Bethlehem some shepherds were guarding their sheep—

**Narrator 2:** In fact, shepherds weren't even welcome in the town. They made people nervous. Not nice types at all. Why do you want to talk about them?

**Narrator 1:** *(Getting angry with Narrator 1, speaking even more loudly.)* One night in the fields near Bethlehem some shepherds were guarding their sheep—

**Narrator 2:** I reckon the less said about those shepherds the better. I heard they weren't even proper shepherds. Those fields near Bethlehem held the sheep for the temple sacrifices. Good as dead, their sheep were. Reckon you're best to forget about those shepherds…

**Narrator 1:** *(Shouting.)* ONE NIGHT IN THE FIELDS NEAR BETHLEHEM SOME SHEPHERDS WERE GUARDING THEIR SHEEP—

**Narrator 2:** Shhh! You'll wake the whole of Bethlehem! And they'll probably blame those shepherds. They get blamed for all sorts of things – litter left by the roadside, vegetables nicked from village gardens…

**Narrator 1:** *(Speaking loudly and quickly.)* ONE NIGHT IN THE FIELDS NEAR BETHLEHEM SOME SHEPHERDS WERE GUARDING THEIR SHEEP AND SUDDENLY THERE WAS A FLASH AROUND THEM AND THE LORD'S ANGEL APPEARED. *(Looking at Narrator 2, slowing down and in a normal voice.)* 'Don't be afraid!' the angel said, 'I bring good news of great joy for everyone. Today in Bethlehem, a Saviour has been born. He's the Promised One, the Christ.'

**Narrator 2:** Is that all?

**Narrator 1:** Not exactly! *(Continuing tentatively.)* 'You will know who he is, because you will find him wrapped in cloths and lying in a manger.'

**Narrator 2:** Who's going to find the Promised One, the Christ?

**Narrator 1:** The shepherds, of course. The angel was talking to the shepherds…

**Narrator 2:** Not those no good…

**Narrator 1:** *(Firmly.)* Suddenly they were surrounded by angels all praising God. They said, 'Praise God in heaven! Peace on earth to everyone who pleases God!'

**Narrator 2:** Peace to everyone who pleases God? Well that counts the shepherds out. No one was ever pleased with the shepherds. They spent so long with their sheep, they smelt like sheep. And I can't imagine the likes of them being interested in God. From what I hear, they didn't keep God's laws or go to the synagogue or anything. They'd need to smarten up before God would be pleased with them! Wouldn't they? Well, wouldn't they?

# Nativity without rehearsal

*A short nativity with one adult reader and at least six 'actors'*

**You will need:** *an improvised manger, some token costumes*

This is a simple drama which can accommodate as many children as you have costumes. Stand the actors in a row at the front. If possible, the angels should stand behind and above the other Bible characters. Assign each actor with their particular verse in the poem. During each verse, the characters described face the congregation. The rest of the time they face backwards. In the final verse, the entire cast faces the front. End the performance by pointing to the manger with Jesus inside.

First there was an angel
who came to Zechariah.
He said his wife Elizabeth
was going to have a child.
Zac did not believe him –
for Elizabeth was too old.
But soon the baby John was born,
just like old Zac was told.

Next the same archangel
came down to cousin, Mary.
She found Archangel Gabriel
really rather scary!
'Don't worry,' said the angel,
'you'll have a baby son.
Call him Jesus, if you please,
he'll be God's chosen one.'

Quick! Send another angel.
Put Joseph's mind at peace!
It wasn't hard for him to guess
the baby wasn't his.
'Don't worry,' said the angel,
'the baby is God's Son.
This is the Messiah,
the prophets said would come.'

At first it was one angel
who flew above the hills.
The shepherds were quite terrified,
stood frozen – very still.
'Don't worry,' said the angel,
'at what I'm going to say.
Good news I tell you! God's own Son
has just been born today.'

Then many, many angels
filled the night-time sky.
'Praise God who sends his Son down from
his heavenly home on high.'
The shepherds rushed to see the child –
he was lying in the hay,

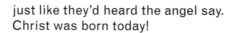

just like they'd heard the angel say.
Christ was born today!

Everyone had troubles,
Everyone had woes.
Just ordinary people,
whom life had dealt a blow.
But faithfully they prayed to God
to keep them in his care.
And God had kept his promise through
the baby lying there.

## Dialogue

*A discussion between Mary and Elizabeth, suitable for young people*

After the performance, you may wish to explain that it wasn't quite like that but if anyone wants to read further they can look it up in Luke 1:26–56.

**Characters:** *Mary, a young girl, dressed in normal teenage clothes (no blue headdress) Elizabeth, an older woman*

**Mary:** Auntie Liz, I'm so worried. The strangest thing happened to me last night.
**Elizabeth:** Whatever is the matter?
**Mary:** I met an angel.
**Elizabeth:** Are you talking about that beautiful boy you met the other day?
**Mary:** No, of course not, Auntie. I'm completely in love with Joseph – I can't wait to get married. *(Starts to cry.)*
**Elizabeth:** Dear, dear, Mary, there's no need to cry.
**Mary:** Yes there is. The angel told me that God would make me pregnant. But Joseph won't believe me, and then I'll be chucked out of our home 'cos he won't marry me and my life will be a complete disaster. *(Crying lots.)*
**Elizabeth:** Now, did this angel say anything else?
**Mary:** Hummmm, yes. He did say that I shouldn't be afraid – what a laugh! And that I'd be giving birth to the Son of God by the power of the Holy Spirit.
**Elizabeth:** Not much, then. Anything else?
**Mary:** The angel said that 'nothing is impossible with God'.
**Elizabeth:** Do you know that I heard a rabbi reading about a son from the line of David who'd be king for ever? The angel didn't mention anything about that, did he?
**Mary:** Now you come to mention it, he did! Is that relevant? I never pay attention to those old rabbis.
**Elizabeth:** Mary, I think you're going to become the most famous woman ever! How exciting is that? You're going to be the mother of God!
**Mary:** Nah, I'm nothing special. I'll just let God use me anyway he likes.

## Good news!

*A quirky insight into the life of the Christmas angels!*

**Characters:** *Angel 1 and Angel 2*

**Props:** two sheets of paper

**Angel 1:** *(To the audience, as if he's just spotted them.)* Yes, I'm an angel! Don't look like one, I know, but we're not meant to, if you know what I mean. We're meant to blend in... I never get to shine and look radiant on earth... *(Sighs.)* To be honest, I feel very depressed. I mean, it's always Gabriel and Michael who get the good jobs, and those seraphs... All I do is zip down to earth and help people not to fall down holes and stuff. Last week I helped stop a car going into a ditch. *(Sighs again.)* I mean, I know it's good and helpful and all that, but – well, to be honest, I'm a bit ambitious. And I feel...
*(Angel 2 walks on, holding a sheet of paper.)*
**Angel 2:** Got something for you, mate.
**Angel 1:** Oh, like what?
**Angel 2:** *(Looks at paper.)* Mmm... Looks like a new assignment.
**Angel 1:** Cool! Perhaps I'm going to be the guardian angel for somebody really important – a prophet, a king...
*(Angel 2 slaps paper into Angel 1's hand.)*
**Angel 1:** *(Reads it.)* Oh no! How boring! Go along with some of the other angels to... Oh, what? Appear to some shepherds! Why would any self-respecting angel want to appear to dirty, smelly shepherds? And say what? *(Continues to read.)* Good news? What good news could God possibly have for those rogues? Suppose we'll have to sit there pretending to be some scruffy travellers, in the middle of some horrible wet field, surrounded by horrible wet sheep...
*(Angel 2 comes by again and slaps another sheet of paper into Angel 1's hand.)*
**Angel 2:** More detail, mate. *(Goes off)*
**Angel 1:** What's this? A note from the Boss? The Boss himself! Wow, perhaps this job is bigger than I thought! *(Reads)* 'Rory, please rehearse this and get it right. It's really important.' Wow! OK... what have I got to say? 'Don't be afraid! I have good news for you, which will make everyone happy. This very day in King David's home town a Saviour was born for you. He is Christ the Lord. You will know who he is, because you will find him dressed in baby clothes and lying on a bed of hay.' I've got to say that? And the others have got to say: 'Praise God in heaven! Peace on earth to everyone who pleases God.' Right! Better go and practice! WOW! I'm allowed to SHINE! *(Excitedly punches air.)* Yes! *(Wanders off saying, 'Don't be afraid... good news.... Saviour born... Christ the Lord.')*

# Bad news, Herod

*A short sketch to introduce the religious and political scene at the time of Jesus' birth*

**Characters:** *Priest and Teacher*

**Teacher:** *(Looking through some scrolls.)* Hmm... Bethlehem?
**Priest:** Uh-huh. Bethlehem. *(Points finger at text.)* That's it. 'Bethlehem... You are very important... From your town will come a leader, who will be like a shepherd for my people Israel...' That's a reference to the Messiah, all right.
**Teacher:** Mmm... Messiah... Mmm... *(Scratches head.)* And these wise men say this child has been born and they know. How?
**Priest:** Star in the east... They saw it... They say it's his star and they want to worship him...
**Teacher:** Well, that's... different! *(Sighs.)* Oh well, we've found out what the King wanted to know. What's he going to do?
**Priest:** Well, let's face it; he isn't going to want any Messiahs around, is he? I mean, doesn't do much for the balance of power, does it? I think he's going to send these wise men off to Bethlehem and they'll find this new king Messiah and then...
**Teacher:** And then?
**Priest:** They'll tell Herod where the boy is and then...
**Teacher:** And then?
**Priest:** Well, he'll go and...
**Teacher:** And?
**Priest:** Well, you know – kill him!
**Teacher:** But the Messiah... He'll be a little child.
**Priest:** Uh-huh. *(They look at each other.)* Well, let's go and tell Herod.
**Teacher:** *(Miserably.)* Can't we emigrate?
**Priest:** Afraid not. Anyway, not sure I want any Messiahs hanging around to rock the boat. Do you?

# News reading

*A short drama with a 'tongue-in-cheek' outcome*

**You will need:** *a desk; a chair; photographic images (from the Internet or magazines) of a famous footballer, a rock group, a film star, a Head of State, an entrepreneur and a newborn baby – either load the images into a PowerPoint slideshow or copy them on to acetate*

Beforehand, ask a volunteer to rehearse the script below and perform it dressed as a newsreader. Prepare a PowerPoint or acetate with the pictures of the characters above so that they can be displayed as each is mentioned in the script. It might be useful to rehearse this for timing.

**Newsreader:** Good morning. Here is today's news. It has been announced that star footballer, [name] is to leave [insert football club he currently plays for] to join a non-league side [insert name of a local amateur club] in a free transfer deal.

Meanwhile rock group, [name] have cancelled their sell-out stadium tour of the US, choosing instead to play a series of free concerts in the back of the hall of [insert name of your church]. The news was the icing on the cake for the church, coming only hours after they heard that they'd successfully secured Hollywood star, [name] for the role of Joseph [or Mary] in their annual nativity play.

And now, royal news. Her Majesty Queen Elizabeth II *[or your own Head of State]* was yesterday spotted at *[insert name of a local second-hand car dealership]*. Her Majesty was agreeing a deal for the dealership to buy the entire fleet of royal *[or state]* cars, having decided that she will in future travel only by public transport.

On to business news. Entrepreneur, *[name]* has announced he is to walk away from his business empire. *[Name]* has told friends that he wants to run the convenience store at *[insert name of local High Street]*.

And finally... Police have said they will take no further action against Mr Ivor Goodnews. They had been questioning Mr Goodnews after receiving reports that he was sending Christmas cards with the statement that the baby in the manger scene pictured on the front of the cards was the Son of God. Explaining the force's decision to reporters, a top officer said, 'We are satisfied that the majority of decent people will recognise the claims of Mr Goodnews about Mary's baby to be so far-fetched as to be incredible and unworthy of further consideration.'

So there you are, don't try and read too much into the traditional Christmas story – just enjoy the sentimentality of that stable scene! We're back at [insert time of next service]. Until then have a great day.

# Find the real king

*Drama for older children and adults*

**Characters:** *The announcer, King Herod, three wise men, Jesus' spokesperson*

**Props:** *a manger with hay and a doll; strong paper crowns for Herod and the wise men to wear, and one to display on the manger*

The actors stand in a row, all in place before the announcer's introduction. Herod is always arrogant and boastful. The wise men are firm and honest but sometimes rather apologetic when they feel they have been misrepresented. Jesus' spokesperson is always decisive but never boastful. There should be a pause between each group of three statements.

**Announcer:** We're so glad to welcome you as the audience for today's edition of the game show, 'Find the Real….' We have several contestants this week and we are looking for the 'Real King'. Our first contestant is King Herod. *(Waves hand in the direction of Herod.)* Next we have the wise men. They are working as a team. *(Wave hand in the direction of the wise men.)* And lastly we have baby Jesus, *(Wave hand towards the manger.)* but as he is fast asleep at the moment his spokesperson will answer on his behalf. A round of applause for all our contestants – but don't wake the baby. As you know, each contestant will have the chance to make their claim to be recognised as the 'Real King'. At the end of the programme you will be asked to decide who the 'Real King' is.

**Herod:** I look like a king.
**Wise men:** We look like kings.
**Jesus' spokesperson:** I look like an ordinary baby.
*(Pause.)*
**Herod:** The Romans made me a king.
**Wise men:** Over the years people have made us into kings.
**Jesus' spokesperson:** I have always been the King.
*(Pause.)*
**Herod:** There has been a lot written about me, most of it probably true.
**Wise men:** There has been a lot written about us, much of it probably untrue.
**Jesus' spokesperson:** There was a lot written about me hundreds of years before I was born, and it is all true.
*(Pause.)*
**Herod:** I am rich and live in a palace, so I must be a king.
**Wise men:** We are rich and come from faraway lands, but that doesn't make us kings.
**Jesus' spokesperson:** I am poor and live in a borrowed house, but that doesn't mean I am not the King.
*(Pause.)*
**Herod:** *(Pointing to self.)* The king is here already.
**Wise men:** We have come to find a more important king.
**Jesus' spokesperson:** Seek and you will find.
*(Pause.)*
**Herod:** I think I am a king.
**Wise men:** *(Pointing at Herod.)* We think he is a king, but he *(Pointing at Jesus.)* is a more important king.
**Jesus' spokesperson:** I am the King of kings.
*(Pause.)*
**Herod:** I am a king. *(Throws his crown down and stamps off.)*
**Wise men:** We are probably not really kings, but we know who is. *(Reverently bow and put their crowns down beside the manger as gifts, then move away.)*
**Jesus' spokesperson:** I Am. *(Spokesperson moves away leaving the manger alone.)*
*(Pause.)*
**Announcer:** Well, it's 'make-your-mind-up' time. Who do you think is the 'Real King' – and why?

# The promised Messiah

*Bible monologues for two readers*

**Characters and scene:** *You will need two reasonable actors to play the parts of Mary and Joseph. Costumes are optional. They sit each side of a large room divider. Light music plays in the background. Each soliloquises.*

**Joseph:** 'I hear that girl of yours is in the family way!' That's what he said – but sneeringly. I nearly hit him. But what's the use? It's a mighty strange thing, this. We've never been alone together… let alone that… You should have heard her father and the rabbi – going on and on… honour of the family… sinning before God… letting the family down. As for her mother… Well, she never stopped! *(Pause.)* I heard this murmur about Isaiah though – about promises. I didn't understand that – can't blame them though. After all, it's mighty strange. But I still love her, you know. When she told me – about the angel and all that – she looked so young… so pretty… so innocent… so holy – really! I believed her… So I said, 'Shalom!' It's our life and we will go ahead. Emmanuel – that's what the angel said – call him Jesus. God is with us… Saviour… Just as he promised. So I will.

**Mary:** It was so hard – telling them about the baby and the angel and everything. I knew they wouldn't believe me to start with. Everybody got in such a state; the rabbi was particularly rude. But then rabbis often are. But inside I felt quite calm. Joseph was too, once he heard from the angel. I'm really glad God reassured him. It's all very strange… Yet underneath it seems so, well, right. So we're carrying on. It's really quite silly, but I just can't stop singing… various bits of the psalms, put together. We'll just have to see what God will do next. Perhaps Elizabeth will have some advice. We'll see.

# Tell me about your vision

*A sketch examining Revelation 1*

**Characters:** *Bernard Brainworthy is a psychiatrist, or therapist for the rich and famous of ancient Greece; he loves tapping his note-taking pencil on his clipboard; John is an elderly disciple, a follower of Jesus, and is widely believed to have written one of the Gospels.*

**Bernard:** So John, please go over that again.
**John:** Well, it's like I said. There I was having a good pray...
**Bernard:** Pray? Oh yes – that's where you believe you're talking to your God. Do carry on.
**John:** I was having a good pray when suddenly I heard a loud voice behind me.
**Bernard:** Now, that was the voice that was a trumpet?
**John:** No, not a trumpet but it sounded like a trumpet. It was so loud and powerful – like an announcement, a herald, like that bit in *Shrek 2* where Shrek and Fiona go to Far Far Away.
**Bernard:** *Shrek 2*?
**John:** Never mind. Anyway, this voice told me to write down everything I saw and send it to seven churches.
**Bernard:** Any particular seven churches?
**John:** Well, yes and no.
**Bernard:** Now, don't be so evasive!
**John:** Well, I'm not. You see, there are seven churches that are mentioned in particular, but...
**Bernard:** Go on. *(Making notes on his clipboard.)*
**John:** But... well, it has something to do with the number seven...
**Bernard:** What? It's your lucky number, the final number in your weekly Grecian Lotto draw?
**John:** No, the number seven signifies something. It's not just a number – it also means being complete.
**Bernard:** *(Very sceptical.)* Rriiigghhhttt...
**John:** So although it was to be sent to seven churches it could also mean that was to be sent to all the churches.
**Bernard:** *(Becoming confused.)* So this vision was to be written and sent to either seven churches or all the churches?
**John:** Well, no. Initially the seven churches that I was told about...
**Bernard:** And who was it talking to you again? A giant walking trumpet? *(He chuckles at his own joke.)*
**John:** *(Looking at Bernard as though he's pathetic.)* No, not a trumpet, seven lampstands! *(Bernard almost falls off his couch and John has a good chuckle at confusing him.)*
**Bernard:** Sorry?
**John:** Well, when I turned around the first thing I saw was seven lampstands, and they were golden – a bit like your tan, although that's a bit more orange.
**Bernard:** Ah, the number seven again! Does that mean they represented all the lamps in the world? Does that mean you saw a very bright light?
**John:** No, I saw seven golden lampstands and they are... well, I'll tell you about that in a minute.
**Bernard:** OK. Why don't we take a five-minute break and then get back to what you saw amongst the lampstands?

# At the Chinese restaurant

*A sketch examining 1 Thessalonians 4:1 – 5:11*

**Scene:** *a couple are sitting at the table of a Chinese restaurant, having finished their meal.*

**One:** *(Pushes his plate away from him, leans back and rubs his full stomach.)* Well, that was a great Chinese meal.
**Two:** Sure was! They really know how to do a mean Cha-Shao Quick-Roast Beef.
**One:** The omelette and chips were good too.
**Two:** *(Looking at One disapprovingly.)* Yeah.
**One:** Just the fortune cookies to open then.
**Two:** If we must.
*(One and Two crack open their cookies. One finds a small note in his and then turns his attention to Two who is unfolding a large piece of paper – actually 1 Thessalonians 4:1 – 5:11.)*
**One:** *(Reading his note, trying not to show his disappointment.)* 'To follow the bottle-nose dolphin, you must launch your boat into the waters.' Hmm, I wonder what that means.
**Two:** Perhaps you're going on a cruise.
**One:** *(Excitedly.)* Do you think so?
**Two:** No!
**One:** Oh! Anyway, what does your cookie say?
*(Two starts to read it to himself, mumbling the occasional word.)*
**One:** No, no! Read it out. I want to hear if you're joining me on my cruise.
**Two:** Well, it tells me that one day I'm going to be with God in heaven, that there'll be all the usual things – you know, trumpet blasts, archangels and the like. And then Jesus will return and take me to his Father.
**One:** Wow! When's that going to happen?
**Two:** It says that no one knows. It will happen totally out of the blue and catch many people unawares, but it will happen, that's for sure.
**One:** How come you get all that and I just get this note about a dolphin?
**Two:** I suppose because I follow Christ. You see, this note is from the Bible. It says that because all those who believe and trust in Jesus will be taken by him to be with God. That's a 100% guarantee.
**One:** *(Blowing his cheeks out.)* I need that, don't I? I don't want a dolphin... or a cruise.
**Two:** *(Pleased at his friend's response.)* That's right, and you can do something about it.
**One:** Yeah, and I know what to do. *(He turns around and clicks his finger in the air.)* Waiter, this cookie's faulty. Can you bring me another?

# The pageant of Christ's nativity

*A pageant, by Steve Dixon (after 'The Pageant of the Shearmen and Tailors of Coventry')*

**Characters:** *Narrator 1, Narrator 2, Narrator 3, Isaiah, Mary, Angel Gabriel, Joseph, Sim (a shepherd), Shepherd 1, Shepherd 2, Angel 1, Angel 2, Angel 3, Angel 4, Calcas (King Herod's Herald), Herod, Wise Man 1, Wise Man 2, Wise Man 3.*

## Prologue

Three narrators enter, carrying large decorated scripts. *(The NARRATORS should be encouraged to learn their lines as far as possible, but can use their scripts for help and to prompt the rest of the cast.)*

**Narrator 1:** Ladies,

**Narrator 2:** gentlemen,

**Narrator 3:** and others,

**Narrator 1:** we are pleased to present –

**Narrator 2:** 'The Pageant of Christ's Nativity'.

**Narrator 1:** The Prologue!

*Isaiah leaps onto the stage to a clash of cymbals.*

**Narrator 3:** That's the bit that comes before the rest of it *(Narrators 1 and 2 glare.)* I'll say no more.

**Isaiah:** My name is Isaiah – a prophet of old.
God's blessing to all! The night is cold.
But I have news to warm your heart,
God offers us a second start.
Although we've lived in misery
Since Adam and Eve ate from the tree.
Behold, a lass shall bear a boy,
Who'll lead us back to grace and joy.
Much more of this I'd like to tell –
But now it's time to bid farewell!

*Isaiah exits, to a clash of cymbals.*

**Narrator 1:** Farewell, Isaiah, and God bless you!

**Narrator 3:** Do all his prophecies come true?

**Narrator 2:** Just give them time. It says down here, *(Points to script.)*
That lad's not due for 700 years!

**Narrator 3:** Time for a song then!

### SONG

*(The songs between the scenes are sung by the congregation or audience. Any Christmas songs*

would be suitable to use, but as this play draws on ancient 'nativity' traditions, it would be a good opportunity to introduce children to some of the riches of the Christmas carol heritage.)*

## Scene one: The Annunciation

**Narrator 1:** And now the time has almost come,
When God will give the world his Son.

*Mary enters.*

**Narrator 2:** Here comes Mary. God loves her well.

*Gabriel with other angels in attendance enter.*

**Narrator 3:** And here's the angel, Gabriel.

**Gabriel:** Hail Mary, full of grace,
The Lord is with you!

**Narrator 3:** Just see her face!

**Mary:** I am amazed! My heart stands still!
God keep me safe from any ill.

**Gabriel:** Mary, you shall have a son.

**Mary:** But I'm not wed! It can't be done!

**Gabriel:** The lad will be the Son of God.

*Mary kneels.*

**Mary:** In that case, I will serve the Lord.

*Gabriel and angels exit.*

**Narrator 1:** The angels go,

**Narrator 2:** And time goes, too.

**Narrator 3:** Mary weds Joseph, her sweetheart true.

*Joseph enters, looking gloomy.*

**Narrator 1:** The happy man is coming – see!

**Narrator 3:** He doesn't look too happy to me.

**Joseph:** I have to go from Galilee
To Bethlehem, my family's place.

**Narrator 1:** The Romans are taxing the whole human race.

**Mary:** I'll come, too. If God takes care
We'll both of us, get safely there.

52

*Mary and Joseph exit.*

**Narrator 2:** The whole of Palestine's travelling today.

**Narrator 3:** Let's sing them on their weary way.

SONG

# Scene two: The shepherds

*Mary and Joseph enter.*

**Narrator 2:** Something we forgot to say –
The baby's nearly on its way.

**Narrator 1:** Joseph sees his wife grow weak
And so that good man starts to speak.

**Joseph:** We still have three more leagues to go.

**Mary:** Joseph, dear, I know – I know!

**Joseph:** Rest awhile – that's what you need –
While I go on at double speed.
I'll book a place to stay the night, dear.

**Mary:** Joseph, night's already here!

*Mary and Joseph exit.*

**Narrator 1:** Mary huddles by a tree –
The stars her only company.
She'll pass the time by counting them
As Joseph runs to Bethlehem.

*Sim, the shepherd enters.*

**Narrator 3:** Who's this fellow? He looks lost.

**Sim:** I'm lost and half dead with the frost.
Not only that, I've lost my sheep –
And both my friends, who also keep
Their flocks upon this ground.

**Narrator 3:** A shepherd, I'll be bound!

**Narrator 1:** *(Glares.)* A shepherd wanders in the night,
Muddled by the lack of light.

**Narrator 2:** He shouts into the chilly air

**Sim:** Eh up, fellers! Are you there?

*Shepherds 1 and 2 enter.*

**Shepherd 1:** That's the voice of brother Sim.

**Shepherd 2:** Come on then, let's go to him.

**Shepherd 1:** Brother, here we are – we've found you.

**Shepherd 2:** Here, Sim, wrap this cloak around you.

**Shepherd 1:** It's gone so far into the night
That soon we'll see the morning light.

**Shepherd 2:** Let's sit and have a little feast
Until the sun climbs in the East.

*They eat.*

**Sim:** Brothers, look into the night.
What is that, that shines so bright?

**Narrator 1:** The heavens shimmer with a star
That outshines all the rest by far.

**Shepherd 1:** This is the time we've heard foretold
When on a night that's freezing cold
A lass will bear a wondrous boy
To fill the world with heaven's joy.

**Sim:** He tells the truth. He is no liar.
I've read about it in Isaiah.

**Narrator 2:** They kneel and pray with all their might
That God will let them see the sight.
Angels sing. The heavens glow.

*Angels enter.*

**Angels:** Gloria, in excelsis deo!

**Narrator 3:** The glory of the Lord shone round
And scared to death, they hugged the ground.

**Angel 1:** Fear not, we bring you news of joy.

**Angel 2:** In Bethlehem is born a boy –

**Angel 3:** A Saviour, who is Christ the Lord.

**Angel 4:** And so you may believe our word –
You'll find him wrapped in strips of cloth,
Laid in a straw-filled feeding trough.

**Angels:** Glory to God! On earth, be peace!
Goodwill to all!

**Narrator 3:** And so they cease.

*Angels exit.*

**Narrator 1:** God's glory dwindles from the skies.

**Narrator 2:** In wonderment, the shepherds rise.

**Sim:** Let's go!

**Shepherd 2:** At once!

**Shepherd 1:** Without delay!
Christ the Lord is born today!

*Shepherds exit, running.*

SONG

## Scene three: The manger

*A manger has been set, with a seat for Mary.*

**Narrator 3:** Mary's had a babe in the straw?
She was under a tree, the last we saw!

**Narrator 1:** *(Glares.)* While simple Sim was chasing sheep,
Joseph found a place to sleep.

**Narrator 2:** Bethlehem was packed and heaving.
Even the inn was full that evening –
Except for a stable round the back.
And there it was, among the tack
And lowing cows with jostling horns
The Saviour of the World was born.

**Narrator 1:** Behold the Holy Family,
With Jesus on his mother's knee.

*Joseph and Mary enter, carrying the baby wrapped in strips of cloth. Mary sits and cradles Jesus. Joseph stands behind her.*

**Joseph:** He might catch a cold.
This place is so bare.
But I couldn't find anything else anywhere.

**Mary:** Dear Joseph, just now, with my baby to hold,
This stable's as bright as a palace of gold.

**Joseph:** But it's packed out with cows. It's smelly and damp.
It's not fit for God's Son. It's not fit for a tramp!

**Mary:** Husband, calm down now! All's as it should be.
Our child has no need of the world's finery.
The glory of Heaven, like a blanket is spread
Wherever this baby lays down his sweet head.

**Joseph:** Can you hear someone, outside by the door?

**Mary:** Only the wind with its rattle and roar.

*The voices of the shepherds can be heard as they approach.*

**Shepherd 1:** You can't give him that, Sim. Most certainly not!

**Sim:** But, brother, I ask you – what else have I got?

**Joseph:** It sounds like somebody's having a row.

**Mary:** Are you sure that it isn't a restless cow?

**Sim:** What shall we do? Shall we go straight on in?

**Joseph:** I'll nip out and check if it is just the wind.

**Narrator 2:** Those faithful shepherds had tramped the town
And searched each alley until they found
A stable that shone in the light of a star.

**Narrator 3:** Their journey's ended, and here they are.

*Joseph leads the shepherds to Mary and Jesus.*

**Shepherd 2:** Greetings Mary, mother mild,
We've brought some presents for your child.

**Sim:** See! Everything's just as the angels said –
There's even a manger, look! That's for his bed.

**Shepherd 2:** *(Offering a pipe.)* Take my good pipe in your hand.
It plays fine tunes. It's really grand.
*(Realising the problem.)* Well, maybe when you've grown a bit.
You'll get as much pleasure as I've had from it.

**Sim:** Now then lad, *(Aside.)* it's just like they said.
Here's a warm hat to put on your head.
The cold will never make you complain,
Nor the wind or the sun, the hail or the rain.

**Joseph:** Thank you, shepherds.

**Mary:** You're very kind.

**Sim:** *(To Shepherd 1.)* You see, I said they wouldn't mind
If the gifts we brought weren't fancy and fine.

**Shepherd 1:** Greetings, Lord of sea and land!
Put my mittens on your hands.
I'm sorry, Lord – I hope you'll see
There's nothing better belongs to me.

*Shepherd 1 kneels and tugs the others down with him.*

**Mary:** Kind shepherds thank you for your call.
I'll pray to God to bless you all
And bring you to heaven on your last day.

**Shepherd 1:** Come on, brothers – we'd best not stay.

*Shepherds exit.*

54

**Narrator 1:** The shepherds left and spread the word
About the things they'd seen and heard
So all of Bethlehem buzzed and wondered,

**Narrator 2:** But Mary kept quiet in her heart and pondered.

*Mary leaves, slowly and thoughtfully, cradling Jesus. Joseph follows, carrying the gifts.*

SONG

# Scene four: Herod the King

**Narrator 3:** And now our story turns about
From a humble prince to a boasting lout,

**Narrator 1:** From brightness when the dark held sway
To darkness in the midst of day,

**Narrator 2:** From Heaven's King in his straw-filled throne
To a king of straw in a golden home,

**Narrator 3:** From Jesus Christ, Emmanuel,
To Herod – a king raised out of Hell!

*Herod enters.*

**Narrator 1:** See where he struts on his palace walls.

*Calcas enters, carrying a grand scroll.*

**Narrator 1:** Below, his herald, Calcas, bawls.

*Trumpet fanfare and drums.*

**Calcas:** *(Reading from the scroll.)* The mightiest conqueror in history –
Herod, your King – has made a decree.
Hear and obey, or die and be damned,
For heaven and earth are at his command.
His fury makes the lightning flash,
The storm clouds roll, and thunders crash.
His bright sword makes the giants quake.
For fear of him the mountains shake.
From north to south his law is heard –
He'll blast the world with just one word.
So hear, you minions, and obey,
The decree King Herod makes this day.
No strangers through his realm may go
Unless they pay for doing so.
Five golden coins at the palace gate –
Or the gallows tree will be your fate!

*Herod and Calcas exit to trumpet fanfare and drums.*

**Narrator 3:** I don't like him. He can't half shout.

*Wise Man 1 enters.*

**Narrator 1:** *(Pointing to Wise Man 1.)*
Shh! There might be spies about!

**Narrator 2:** He's someone special from the East.

**Narrator 3:** Are you sure? He's all crumpled and creased!

**Narrator 1:** *(Glares.)* When Jesus was born in Bethlehem
There came wise men to Jerusalem.
Stained with travel, they'd come from afar,
Guided by prophecy, seeking a star.

**Wise Man 1:** Praise God! At last, a bright star shines,
That heralds a babe from Jesse's line.
Now the promised time has come
And God has given us his Son.

*Wise Man 2 enters.*

**Narrator 2:** *(Pointing to Wise Man 2.)* How many lands has this man crossed?

**Narrator 3:** I'd say, like simple Sim, he's lost!

**Wise Man 2:** Now God that made me,
give some clue –
So many realms I've travelled through,
That where I am, I've no idea.
But look – another wise man's here.
Most noble friend, will you please say
What purpose leads you on this way?

**Wise Man 1:** God's chosen holy child I seek –
The one of whom the prophets speak.

**Wise Man 2:** Then may I travel on with you?
I'm searching for that infant, too.

*Wise Man 3 enters.*

**Narrator 1:** Here comes another learned vagrant.
He needs a wash – he's none too fragrant!

**Wise Man 3:** *(Praying.)* Lord of heaven, send me a guide –
I've travelled dale and mountain side
Until all lands look just the same.
I pray you, tell this country's name.

**Narrator 3:** These men are good at prophecy,
But not too hot on geography!

**Wise Man 3:** Behold – two wise men now appear!
Good sirs, what are you doing here?

**Wise Man 1:** We seek the child whose birth is told
By yonder star that shines like gold.

**Wise Man 3:** The very same I've come to see.
Please may I join your company?

*The Wise Men exit.*

**Narrator 1:** And so he joins the learned band.
But soon they are in Herod's land –
Strangers who owe five coins of gold.

**Narrator 3:** They'd better pay, or heads will roll!

**Narrator 2:** Stranger strangers you never saw,
So when they reach the palace door
Calcas questions them in turn.
Their stories cause him deep concern.

*Calcas enters from one side, with the Wise Men behind him. Herod enters from the other side.*

**Calcas:** Hail, my Lord! Three men I bring,
Who claim they seek another king.
A king who is a child, they say,
But who will rule the world some day.

**Herod:** WHAT?

*Calcas motions to show him that the Wise Men are behind him and Herod becomes all smiles.*

**Herod:** Welcome, friends. Come forward, please.
Don't be afraid. Be at your ease.
The mighty shrink when I am furious,
But you bring news that makes me... curious.
A simple favour's all I ask –
When you've succeeded in your task,
Come back and tell me all you know
About this child – for I would go
And pay a special homage, too.

**Wise Man 1:** My Lord, your bidding we will do.

**Herod:** Tell me, when was this baby born?

**Wise Man 2:** Twelve days ago, before the dawn.

**Herod:** Where has this king begun his days?

**Wise Man 3:** In Bethlehem, the prophet says.

**Herod:** Free passage for a hundred days,
I grant you. Go and give your praise –
But do remember what I said.

*The Wise Men exit, bowing.*

**Herod:** When they return, cut off their heads
And strike this upstart infant dead!

**SONG**

# Scene five: Epiphany

**Narrator 1:** And now once more, let's turn our mind
To a king, who is both mighty and kind,

**Narrator 3:** Who's come to stand up for the weak,

**Narrator 2:** A humble child, whom wise men seek.

*Mary enters, carrying Jesus.*

**Narrator 1:** Mary now is fit and strong.

**Narrator 2:** The Holy Child is coming along.

*Joseph enters.*

**Narrator 3:** Joseph's paid his tax to Rome
And soon they'll all be going home.

**Joseph:** Wife, we're ready to leave at your pleasure.

**Mary:** I hope you've packed the shepherds' treasure.

**Joseph:** The pipe, the mittens and the hat?
I've taken extra care of that.

**Mary:** Then make this night our final one
And in the morning we'll be gone.

*The Wise Men enter.*

**Narrator 2:** Just in time, the weary three
Arrive for the Epiphany.

**Narrator 1:** Three wise men of the world bow down
Before the power of Heaven's crown.

*Drums and trumpets – the Wise Men offer their gifts in turn and kneel.*

**Wise Man 1:** Hail Lord, who made the world of old!
In token of Kingship – a cup full of gold.

**Wise Man 2:** Hail to the Lord of highest magnificence!
To mark your priesthood – a cup full of incense.

**Wise Man 3:** Hail Lord, whom God our Father gave us!
Myrrh for the death by which you'll save us.

**Mary:** God grant you, wise men, a just reward
For travelling so far to greet your Lord.
Forgive us if now we retire for the night –
Our journey is long and we leave at first light.

*Mary exits with Jesus, and Joseph carrying the gifts. The Wise Men speak as they walk in the opposite direction.*

**Wise Man 1:** Friends, we have said we'll go back to King Herod.

**Wise Man 2:** For the sake of our honour, we must keep our word.

**Wise Man 3:** But night has now fallen. My feet are like lead.
So let's use this grassy bank as our bed.

*The Wise Men lie down to sleep.*

**Narrator 3:** They can't go back! Please, someone stop them!
That wicked King Herod is going to chop them,
And Jesus too! I just can't look!

**Narrator 2:** Don't worry about it! *(Pointing to script.)* Read on in the book.

**Narrator 1:** *(Reading.)* While the wise men slept on the ground,
The Heavenly Host shone all around.

*The Angels enter.*

**Angel 1:** O wise men from the East, arise!

**Angel 2:** King Herod wove a web of lies.

**Angel 3:** To his palace don't return.

**Angel 4:** The tyrant's heart like hellfire burns!

**Angel 1:** Travel quickly! Journey West!

**Angel 2:** Enough of dozing, sleep and rest!

*The angels exit. The Wise Men rise.*

**Wise Man 1:** Awake, dear friends – I've had a dream.

**Wise Man 2:** I spoke with angels, so it seemed.

**Wise Man 3:** They bade us take the westward way
Or by false Herod be betrayed.

**Wise Man 2:** He mustn't find out who we are –

**Wise Man 3:** We'll melt away with the morning star!

*The Wise Men leave in different directions.*

**Narrator 3:** What about Mary? She needs warning –
They'll be sitting ducks on the road next morning!

**Narrator 2:** The angels will do it – never fear.
In Joseph's dreams they will appear.

*Joseph enters to a crash of cymbals, calling off stage.*

**Joseph:** Wake up Mary! Wake up quick!
Herod's going to play a trick!

*Mary enters, half asleep.*

**Mary:** Come back to sleep – it's dead of night.

**Joseph:** I've seen an angel – we must take flight!

**Mary:** We're leaving tomorrow. Come back to bed.

**Joseph:** If we wait till then, we'll all be dead.
Herod wants to kill the child –
His jealous heart has sent him wild.
We must dash to Egypt before the day.

**Mary:** Come on then, husband – fly away!

*Mary and Joseph exit.*

**Narrator 3:** Let's all shout, 'Hip, hip,

**Narrators:** Hurray!'

*Drums and cymbals*

**Narrator 2:** Friends, our story now is told –
A tale of joy in winter's cold.

**Narrator 1:** Herod died, as tyrants will.

**Narrator 2:** But Christ returned!

**Narrator 3:** He's with us still!

**SONG**

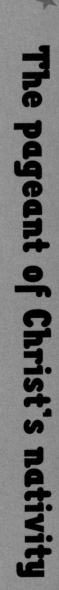

**The pageant of Christ's nativity**

## Angel gazing

*Luke 1:8–20 for three voices*

**Narrator:** Zechariah and Elizabeth were an elderly married couple, both from distinguished priestly families. They lived good lives, following God's rules. Sadly, they had never been able to have children. It seemed impossible now that they would ever have a family, because Elizabeth was quite old.

Zechariah had duties to do as a priest, and he was chosen, by lot, to burn incense on the altar in the temple – a great privilege and possibly a 'once-in-a-lifetime' event.

But while he was there, totally unexpectedly, the angel Gabriel appeared to him by the altar. Zechariah was paralysed with fear!

**Gabriel:** Don't be afraid, Zechariah! God himself has heard your prayers. You and Elizabeth are going to have a baby. Call him John. He is going to be a man of God, who will do great things. He will bring you both – and many other people – much joy. From the moment of his birth he'll be filled with the Holy Spirit of God. His special work will be to call people, even the most hard-hearted, back to knowing God, just like the great prophet Elijah did. He'll prepare the way for God.

**Zechariah:** How can I possibly believe this! My wife and I – well, we're far too old to have a child!

**Gabriel:** I am Gabriel, come to you from the very presence of God. Because you have not believed my message you'll be unable to say a word until the day of your son's birth.

**Narrator:** Everything happened exactly as the angel of the Lord said it would. Zechariah couldn't speak when he came out of the temple and everyone waiting there knew that he had seen a vision. It wasn't long before Elizabeth was overjoyed to find that she had become pregnant.

## Life-changing words

*Isaiah 7:10–14; Luke 1:26,27 for up to six voices*

The following can be read out by one person but is divided into six parts to provide a variety of voices. While the words of the Magnificat are being read, three images could be presented using the OHP or PowerPoint.

**Leader:** Over 700 years before the birth of Jesus, the prophet Isaiah said:
**Reader 1:** *(Reads the words of Isaiah 7:10–14 and pauses.)*
**Leader:** Like all people, Isaiah died, but God did not forget.
**Reader 2:** *(Reads the words of Luke 1:26,27 and pauses.)*

Three female voices should then read out the Magnificat (Luke 1:47–56) one verse at a time. Thus: voice 1, voice 2, voice 3, voice 1, voice 2, voice 3. This would mean that the different voices read the following verses while at the same time the related image is projected on the screen:

**Voice 1:** verses 47,50,53 *(Image 1 – Mary.)*
**Voice 2:** verses 48,51,54 *(Image 2 – collage of world leaders.)*
**Voice 3:** verses 49,52,55 *(Image 3 – aid work in developing country.)*

Alternatively, ask three teenage girls to read the Magnificat. As they read, encourage people to close their eyes and to listen as if this is the first time that they have heard these words. As they do so, they should ask themselves on what was Mary's strong faith in God based. Tell people that at the end there will be a short period of silence. These words have been understood by Christians to be revolutionary and life changing and their meaning should be pondered on.

## Arise, shine!

*Isaiah 60:1–6 for three voices and with a congregational response*

This reading has echoes of the visit of the Magi to Jesus. Reader 2 should be female and reader 3, male.

**Reader 1:** Arise, shine!
**Reader 2:** Shine!
**Reader 3:** Shine!
**All:** Shine, shine, shine!
**Reader 1:** Shine, Jerusalem, for your light has come, and the glory...
**Reader 3:** Glory!
**Reader 2:** Glory!
**All:** Glory!
**Reader 1:** The glory of the Lord has risen upon you!
**All:** Upon you!
**Reader 3:** For darkness shall cover the earth,
**Reader 2:** And thick darkness the peoples;
**Reader 1:** But the Lord will arise upon you...
**All:** Upon you.

**Reader 1:** And his glory will appear over you...
**All:** Over you.
**Reader 1:** Nations shall come to your light;
**Reader 2:** And kings to the brightness of your dawn.
**Reader 3:** Lift up your eyes and look around...
**All:** Around, around.
**Reader 1:** Lift up your eyes and look around!
**Reader 2:** They all gather together, they come to you...
**All:** To you.
**Reader 1:** Your sons shall come from far away...
**Reader 3:** From far away...
**Reader 2:** And your daughters shall be carried on their nurses' arms,
**Reader 1:** Then you shall see and be radiant...
**All:** Radiant!
**Reader 1:** Your heart shall thrill and rejoice...
**All:** Rejoice!
**Reader 1:** Because the abundance of the sea shall be brought to you...
**All:** To you.
**Reader 1:** The wealth of the nations shall come to you;
**Reader 2:** A multitude of camels shall cover you.
**Reader 3:** The young camels of Midian and Ephah; all those from Sheba shall come.
**Reader 1:** They shall bring gold and frankincense, and shall proclaim the praise of the Lord.
**All:** Proclaim the praise of the Lord!

## God with us

*Extracts from Isaiah 9:2,6 and Matthew 1:18–21,23 for four voices*

*(Do not hurry through, even if there are only one or two words in the line.)*

**Voice 1:** The people who walked in darkness
**Voice 2:** Have seen a great light.
**Voice 1:** They lived in a land of shadows,
**Voice 2:** But now, light is shining on them.
**Voice 1:** What is that saving light?
**Voice 2:** A child is *born* to us!
**Voice 1:** A son is *given* to us!
**Voice 2:** He will be called, 'Wonderful Counsellor,'
**Voice 1:** 'Mighty God,'
**Voice 2:** 'Eternal Father,'
**Voice 1:** 'Prince of Peace.'
**Voice 3:** His mother Mary was engaged to Joseph, but before they were married, she found out she was going to have a baby by the Holy Spirit.
**Voice 4:** Joseph was a man who always did what was right, but he did not want to disgrace Mary publicly; so he made plans to break the engagement privately.
**Voice 3:** While he was thinking about this, an angel of the Lord appeared to him in a dream and said:
**Voice 4:** 'Joseph, do not be afraid to take Mary to be your wife. For it is by the Holy Spirit that she has conceived.
**Voice 3:** 'She will have a son, and you will name him Jesus – because he will save his people from their sins.
**Voice 4:** '...and he will be called Immanuel (which means "God is with us").'

### Mary's story

*Luke 2:1–7 retold for younger children*

**You will need:** *a headdress, a baby doll wrapped in pieces of cloth; optional props including a dolls' cot or cradle, baby's or doll's clothes, bread, cheese and a piece of material tied up inside another piece of material, a manger or box of hay*

Dress up as Mary with a simple piece of material tied around your head. Hold the baby doll as you tell the story in the character of Mary, using any of the props you have.

How do you like my baby? He's very special. Of course all babies are special, but this one is extra special. He should have had a special birth really. But it turned out to be very ordinary. Let me tell you about it.

I was very excited when the angel came and told me that I was going to have a baby. And it wasn't going to be just any baby. He would be God's Son! Imagine that!

Joseph, my husband, and I spent a long time getting ready for the baby. I made some little clothes and Joseph carved a beautiful cradle. We wanted the best for this special baby.

There was one thing worrying me though. Joseph told me we would have to go on a journey to Bethlehem. We got ready to go and packed some food and warm cloaks to wrap ourselves up with at night. It was a long journey and took us several days.

At last we reached Bethlehem. There were so many people there it was hard to find somewhere to stay, so we slept in a place where animals are kept.

My baby, God's baby, was born while we were staying there. It wasn't quite the special birth I had hoped for. We wrapped the baby in these strips of cloth, just like any ordinary baby. We didn't have Joseph's beautiful cradle so we just had to make do with a manger, and laid him on the hay that the animals were supposed to eat. We called the baby, 'Jesus'.

God's special baby didn't get the special treatment we were hoping for. But maybe that was just as well. This way Jesus knows what it is like to be ordinary. But he also knows what it is like to be loved. And just looking at him you can tell that he is special. When I look at his shining face, I feel such joy and love. He lights up my life. It feels like a new day is dawning.

### Mary

*A monologue based on Luke 2:16–20 – original text by Michael Wells and adapted by Christine Wright*

Someone knocked, so gently I hardly heard it. I didn't say anything, then the door slowly crept open, and they pushed him in, the young one. He stood there, framed against the starlight and peered in. There was only the one little lamp, glowing golden on a ledge. The opened door made a draught, and the shadows danced and shifted. He jerked forward, propelled by someone's big hand, I think, and as he stood there the other heads peered round him. It was quite comical to see them, but I didn't laugh; they were so shy. I wasn't the only one awake now; Joseph was half asleep, but ready to leap up at any time and protect us. I just smiled, to show they were welcome, and they slowly came forward.

Some of the animals stirred, disturbed by this intrusion. This made one of the men jump, then he went red, ashamed to show fear in front of his work mates. He swaggered a bit, just to show he wasn't afraid, but no one took any notice at all. We were surrounded by now – some on their knees, others peering over shoulders, and the young one with mouth open, just gawping. There was a sort of gasp from all of them. Then the oldest, the one who reminded me so much of Grandfather, asked if we believed in angels. We smiled back our answer; we knew, we all knew. We had something in common.

Wordlessly, I held out my bundle. With real reverence one of them held him, cradled him. A tiny fist opened and fingers grasped at a hairy face. Tears flowed as I lay back and saw my child, being passed from hand to hand, some awkward, some practised. But there was peacefulness, and joy.

It may seem strange to say it, but once I let go I didn't feel quite so lonely. I know I was emotional and tired and all that, but when I shared him with those men, I felt better. It was almost as if he was accepted, he wasn't just my, our, responsibility. These ordinary people had welcomed him. They made a strange picture: coarse clothes, dirty faces, straggling hair, untidy beards, all with a slightly soppy expression on their faces. It was like having our own set of uncles and cousins, ready to protect him; looking out for him.

# Shepherds included

*An interactive version of Luke 2:8–20*

Encourage everyone to respond to the bold words with the following actions and words:

**Shepherds** – turn head away, 'Yuck!'

**Angel** or **angels** – astonished expression, 'Praise God!'

**Sheep** – fluff hair, 'baa'

**Good news** – shout 'Hooray!'

Practise the responses before you start.

**Shepherds** guarded the **sheep** in the fields. Well, someone had to do it. They had a bad reputation, these **shepherds**. They wouldn't keep all the temple laws, so they couldn't worship God there. They found themselves not really fitting in anywhere. They didn't go into the town much or have other friends, these **shepherds**. And people certainly didn't come to visit them. As they spent all day in the fields looking after the **sheep**, they didn't smell too good, and people thought they were stupid, anyway, as they hadn't gone to school.

One night, as usual, they were in the fields guarding the **sheep**. Suddenly, out of the blue, right in front of them, came an **angel**.

'Oooooooooooh!' said the **shepherds**.

'Don't be frightened!' said the **angel**. 'I'm here with **good news** for you, **good news** which will make everyone very happy. I've come to tell you that a saviour has been born for you. He's the Promised One. You'll know who he is because you'll find him lying in a manger.'

A saviour for them! This was very **good news**! And with that the whole sky seemed full of **angels**. They sang, 'Praise God in heaven! Peace on earth to everyone who pleases God.' Then all was quiet again, and all that was left in the fields were the **shepherds** and the **sheep**.

'Let's go and see if we can find this saviour,' they said, and they hurried off and found Mary and Joseph. And there with them was the baby, lying in a manger.

Mary and Joseph were hardly expecting to be visited by **shepherds**! How would **shepherds** have found out the **good news** about their baby? They were very surprised to hear that an **angel** had announced the birth of their baby to these people out in the fields. And of course, Mary and Joseph weren't the only ones who were surprised about the people who were told

first. The **shepherds** were, too. As they went back to their **sheep**, they praised God for the **good news** of Jesus' birth.

# Magi journal

*An account based on Matthew 2:1–12 for young people and adults*

I thought it best to recount the amazing events that have happened over the last few years. It all started when we noticed a new bright star to the west. I am one of the royal courtiers who specialise in making predictions for portents in the sky. In the past we have noticed that events that have happened in our kingdom have been linked with events in the sky, the position of the stars and other stellar events.

Anyway, this bright new star seemed different both in its position and its appearance, and after consulting with my fellow star gazers we decided that it must mean the birth of a new king. So we set out with gifts to pay homage to the new king, following the direction of the star.

The journey led us to Israel, the land of the Jews. They are an interesting people who believe in only one God who created everything. Many of our people worship the sun, the moon and any number of wooden gods. Anyway, once in Israel we went to visit King Herod, who was in Jerusalem, because we were now sure that the star meant a new king.

But when we told Herod, he went very quiet and he seemed worried. Apparently there was no heir to the throne. He called in his religious advisors who told us that the Jews are waiting for someone they call, the Messiah. This Messiah is God's chosen one, who will set everyone free, or something. I didn't catch it all. Herod believed that the star could be the signal that the Messiah had been born. They checked their holy book for references to the birthplace and found that it was to be in Bethlehem, a town just south-west of Jerusalem.

Then something else that was strange happened. As we were preparing to leave, Herod called us to him and asked us to find the location of the child so that he could go and pay his respects. However, the look in his eyes made me feel uneasy. I wasn't sure why, but looking back I now know that he was lying.

We left and followed the star to Bethlehem, and there we found the child. And this I really can't explain! As I looked at the child I knew that this was a special person – was it something in his eyes? I am not sure. But I felt compelled to worship him. This was God's chosen one!

That night I had a very strange dream. It was as if someone with great authority was speaking to me directly and warning me not to go back to Herod. So we left by another route. Halfway through our journey home, news reached us of how deceitful Herod had been. He had worked out how old the child was from the date the star had appeared and how long our journey had taken. And then... he killed all the children of that age in Bethlehem.

I only hope that the child managed to escape. Perhaps the God who had warned me not to tell Herod had also warned the parents of the child. Perhaps I need to find out more about this God and his chosen one.

## Here at last!

*A monologue based on Matthew 2:1–12*

'Here at last,' we said. What a relief it was. The moment I saw the palace roofs I said, 'Yes, this must be the place.'

So we gathered – all of us (the other two and all the drivers, camels and all) – at the golden gate to the palace. It was really rather surprising. Disturbing really – all the guards looked so stern and serious. An ominous feeling settled on each of us. We changed. We put on our best robes. Here we were – three 'kings', rather creased, to see the newborn King.

We waited ages; no one dared to move until he was there. Eventually he appeared. But it wasn't *him*. It was Herod – surrounded by his women, his court, and his 'yes-men'. I felt they rather looked down on us – simply didn't appreciate how far we'd come. Yet for all that, the moment we said why we'd come, everything changed.

'A new king?' he questioned. Then he asked, 'Do you know where he is to be born?'

As if his prophets hadn't already said. There was a great deal of whispering, and then Herod looked more and more angry. So when he sent us off to find the child I was quite relieved. He's a sly old dog, that Herod. And as for coming back to tell him where we'd found the baby – so *he* could worship him, he said – a likely story!

So, off we went to Bethlehem. The star was still up there. Even brighter it seemed to me. I was full of optimism that things would change.

We found him at last. The glory all around – and we gave him gifts: gold, frankincense and myrrh. But we never went back to Herod. Not likely.

# The mince pie tooth

*A modern day story for Christmas, by Marjory Francis*

Storytelling tip: if you're able to show Christmas cards with shepherds on, this would add to the story. You could set up a small display of these cards in the place where you'll be telling the story.

It was the mince pie that did it! One bite into Granny's golden pastry and the tooth jumped out of Jake's mouth and dropped with a 'clink' onto the plate. Jake looked at it in astonishment. He had known that his tooth was wobbly but he hadn't expected it to come out so soon.

'That's done it,' said Lydia. 'You won't be able to be in the Christmas play now. They won't want a shepherd with an ugly face.'

'I will thtill be a thepherd,' insisted Jake.

'Huh, you can't even talk properly now,' said Lydia.

'Yeth I can!' shouted Jake.

'Lydia,' warned Dad, 'don't tease. You know it's perfectly normal for front teeth to fall out when you're about six. Yours did.' Dad called Jake over.

'Come here, old man. Let's have a look at that gap. Wow! I reckon Miss Thompson will put you on the front row of the shepherds with that smile!'

Nobody had noticed Barney licking his lips and wagging his tail, but Lydia thought she'd better make up for being nasty to Jake, so she picked up the empty plate from the floor where it had fallen, and took it out to the kitchen.  She dusted the crumbs into the bin and put the plate in the sink.

'Thank you, darling,' said Mum.

'Jake's tooth's come out,' remarked Lydia.

'Has it?' said Mum. 'Jake! Let's see your tooth.'

'It's here, Mum,' said Jake, running into the kitchen and grinning widely. 'I bit into a mince pie and it came out.'

'I can see the gap,' smiled Mum, 'but where's the tooth?'

'Oh, I forgot. It fell on the plate.' Jake ran back to the sitting room and looked round, while Mum and Lydia looked at each other in dismay.

'Oh dear,' said Mum quietly. 'It must have gone down the plughole.'

Dad gulped. He found the quiet evening he'd been looking forward to was changing into one which involved unscrewing pipes, taking things to pieces and, if he wasn't careful, a flood in the kitchen before he got them together again.

'Are you sure you need this tooth?' asked Dad.

'Yes,' insisted Jake. 'I want to show it to Miss Thompson.'

'Well, I suppose it's a good opportunity to clean this sink pipe out properly,' said Dad, bravely poking a finger into some rather nasty looking gunge he'd found, 'but there's no sign of your tooth, Jake. It was probably washed away.'

Jake's eyes began to fill with tears. He discovered he was really missing his tooth, and he did want to show it to Miss Thompson.

Suddenly Lydia said, 'Wait a minute. I put the crumbs from the plate into the bin. Perhaps Jake's tooth fell in there and not down the sink.'

Everyone looked at everyone else. No one wanted to look in the bin! Eventually Mum took a deep breath and rolled up her sleeves. It was unbelievable what she tipped out of the bin onto a plastic bag – sticky apple cores, slimy banana skins, 'quickly-on-the-way-to-being-mouldy' carrot and potato peelings, all mixed up with messy baked bean tins and the screwed-up (and very smelly) paper that had been wrapped round yesterday's fish and chips. Also there were some chewed-looking chicken bones (Barney hovered round hopefully, but Mum shooed him away.), a few old letters, and some very dead chrysanthemums.

'Is it there? Is it there?' asked Jake, bouncing up and down beside Mum. Mum gingerly lifted up the last slimy banana skin. No tooth was lurking underneath. Jake's face fell. He looked as if he was about to cry.

Lydia was staring at all the rubbish with a thinking look on her face.

'Did you eat the mince pie, Jake?' she asked.

'No, I only bit it,' he said.

'Then where is it,' asked Lydia, 'if it's not in the bin?'

'Barney!' Everyone's eyes turned to look accusingly at the dog, who was looking as if he hadn't eaten anything for hours.

'If Barney ate the mince pie, perhaps he swallowed the tooth as well,' said Lydia.

Jake burst into tears. 'Barney's eaten my tooth! He's a horrible dog!' he wailed. 'I wanted to take my tooth to school to show Miss Thompson and Barney's eaten it.'

Mum gave Jake a big cuddle. 'Oh darling, what a thing to happen! Let's hope Barney doesn't get tummy ache if he has swallowed it.'

Jake began to wail. He didn't care if Barney had tummy ache. It would serve him right! Everything had gone wrong. He knew he wouldn't enjoy being in the Christmas play without his tooth. It wasn't fair! He sobbed for a long time.

Nothing anyone said seemed to help, so Mum just sat with him on her lap, while Dad and Lydia went into the kitchen to scoop the mess back into the rubbish bin. Lydia turned on the tap to wash her chicken-boney and baked-beany hands, but unfortunately Dad hadn't fixed the pipe under the sink yet. The water ran straight out on the kitchen floor.

'I hope that dog's not expecting a Christmas present from me,' said Dad, 'because at the moment I don't feel like giving him one!'

By the time the kitchen was all clean again, Jake had calmed down a bit. Mum asked him to help her arrange the Christmas cards along the mantelpiece, and they looked at each one carefully as they put it in place.

'They look lovely,' said Dad, coming in. 'I see you've put all the ones with shepherds at the front.'

'Dad,' asked Jake, 'did the real shepherds have teeth?'

'Yes, I'm sure they did,' smiled Dad. 'Well, some of the old ones didn't perhaps. People weren't able to look after their teeth in those days as well as we can today, and sometimes when they got old, their teeth would fall out.'

Jake frowned. He didn't want to look like an old shepherd.

'What about Jesus? Did he have teeth?'

'He wouldn't have when he was a baby,' said Dad. 'Babies aren't usually born with teeth. But then he would have grown some little ones like you and when he was about six they would have fallen out, just like yours did.'

'Bedtime, I think,' said Mum, hastily changing the subject, 'can't have you all dozy at the Christmas play tomorrow!'

'Come on, old man,' said Dad. 'I'll take you up and read you a story. Let's put your slippers on.'

Jake sleepily pulled on his rabbit slippers. 'Ouch, there's a stone in this one,' he said. Mum felt inside – and brought out a little pearly tooth!

Jake was tucked up cosily in bed. Everything was all right now. The tooth, which Barney must have knocked into the slipper when he ate the mince pie, was safely in an envelope in his school bag, ready for him to show Miss Thompson. How pleased she would be to see it! Then he thought of his shepherd costume, hanging on the string across the classroom with all the others, waiting for him to dress up for the Christmas play. He imagined himself standing on the stage with all the other shepherds and singing the song about baby Jesus. Everyone would see the gap where his tooth had been, but perhaps he didn't care.

Jake remembered about Jesus being a real little boy like him and having teeth that fell out, and he smiled.

'Dad,' he said, 'it was the mince pie that made my tooth come out. I wonder if Jesus ate mince pies.'

Jake giggled at the thought. Dad grinned too, and then they both laughed for a long time. At last Jake snuggled contentedly down under the duvet.

'Thank you, Jesus, for teeth, and shepherds – and for mince pies,' said Jake. 'Goodnight, Dad.'

# Creative prayer

## God is great!

*Action prayer for younger children*

Remind the children of what the shepherds did when they heard a surprising message from the angels. Do these actions, as you talk about each one:

They heard the angels' message. *(Cup ear.)*
They ran to find Jesus. *(Run on the spot.)*
They saw baby Jesus. *(Shade eyes with hand.)*
And they praised God. *(Raise arms in the air and shout 'God is great!')*

Say that we can join in with the shepherds by copying their actions. Pray:

Dear God, we have heard the surprising message that Jesus was born as a baby in a stable. *(Cup ear.)*
We are so excited that we hurry to praise you. *(Run on the spot.)*
We see pictures of the Christmas story *(Shade eyes.)*
And we are so excited, we want to praise you! *(Raise arms and shout 'God is great!')*

## Praise dance

*A chanted prayer with dance movements*

Form a circle with everyone holding hands. Sing or shout:

Thank you, thank you, Father God, *(Take four steps to the left.)*
You have sent your only son. *(Take four steps to the right.)*
Baby Jesus, now he's here, *(Stand still, rocking your arms.)*
Born to save everyone. *(Point to everyone in the circle.)*

## Here is the baby

*A reflective prayer for younger children*

**You will need:** *quiet, reflective music*

Say the following rhyme with the children:

Here are the shepherds, watching, waiting. *(Hold up fingers on right hand.)*
Here is the angel, shining, showing. *(Hold up index finger on left hand.)*
Here are the shepherds, trembling, shaking. *(Wiggle fingers on right hand.)*
Here are the angels, singing, praising. *(Open and close fingers on left hand like a flash.)*
Here are the shepherds, hurrying, scurrying. *(Move right hand quickly.)*
Here is the baby, lying, sleeping. *(Index finger on left hand, pointing horizontally.)*
Here are the shepherds, rejoicing, praising. *(Open and close fingers on right hand like a flash.)*
Here is Mary, pondering, wondering. *(Hold up little finger on left hand.)*

Repeat the rhyme, but this time end with a time of silence, or play some quiet music. Encourage the children to be quiet and think about the story, just like Mary, wondering and worshipping.

## Our God is here!

*A responsive prayer*

Start by speaking softly and build up to a crescendo.

**Leader:** We have good news for all people.
**All:** Our God is here!
**Leader:** We'll shout it from the mountain tops.
**All:** Our God is here!
**Leader:** We'll shout it from the valleys.
**All:** Our God is here!
**Leader:** We want everyone to know.
**All:** Our God is here!
**Leader:** God is with us today.
**All:** Our God is here!

## Sharing the good news

*A prayer for those who don't yet know Jesus*

**You will need:** *a doll wrapped in swaddling clothes (bandages), some slips of paper large enough to write a name on*

As you hold the doll representing the baby Jesus, remind everyone that the shepherds were so excited by what they saw and heard, that they told the good news of Jesus to everyone they met. Jesus wants everyone to be his friend and wants us to share with others the excitement of being his friend. Sometimes it is difficult because we don't know what to say or we get worried that our friends will laugh at us. But God promises to give us the courage to do this, if we ask him.

Give each person three slips of paper and ask them to write on each one the name of a friend or draw a friend who doesn't yet know Jesus. As they quietly tuck the papers into the folds of Jesus' swaddling, they or you can pray that God will give us all the courage to share his love and joy with the people we love.

## Acrostic prayer

*A prayer activity for older children*

**You will need:** *a large sheet of paper, felt-tip pens*

Write the letters of the word 'Christmas' down the side of the sheet.

Talk about Christmas, and what things the children associate with this time of year, such as presents, food, cards, carols, and so on. Why do we have all these things? What are we really celebrating?

Ask the children to suggest things beginning with any of the letters of the word 'Christmas' that are about the real meaning of Christmas. (Use Bible verses to give them clues.)

If appropriate, use this example, if you get stuck:

**C**hrist (Luke 2:11)
**H**oly (Luke 1:35)
**R**ule (Micah 5:4)
**I**mmanuel (Matthew 1:23)
**S**hepherds (Luke 2:8)
**T**reasure (Matthew 2:11)
**M**ary (Luke 1:27)
**A**ngels (Luke 2:15)
**S**aviour (Luke 2:11)

Invite each of the children to choose one of the words and turn it into a prayer of thanks to God for sending Jesus at Christmas.

## Let the light shine

*A responsive prayer for young people, adults or all ages together*

In the beginning the earth was dark.
*Let the light shine.*
You spoke and the light came.
*Let the light shine.*
Everything that was created received its life from you.
*Let the light shine.*
The light keeps shining in the darkness.
*Let the light shine.*
The darkness has never put it out.
*Let the light shine.*
In the dark places of the world,
*Let the light shine.*
In the dark places of our minds,
*Let the light shine.*
In all we say, think and do,
*Let the light shine.*
Lord Jesus, Light of the world,
*Let the light shine.*

# Pebbles prayer

*A prayer activity for all ages*

**You will need:** *small pebbles for everyone, felt-tip pens, manger, a soundtrack of waves or quiet music*

Beforehand place a pebble and a felt-tip pen under every seat. Place the manger in a prominent and accessible position at the front of the room.

Ask everyone to pick up the pebbles from underneath their seats. Then invite everyone to close their eyes and to move their pebbles around in their hands, feeling its smoothness. Play the waves soundtrack or music in the background as they do this and talk quietly about how the smoothness of the pebbles is the result of years of shaping by the sea.

Read Luke 3:4–6, which uses words from Isaiah to describe John's work of getting people ready for Jesus in terms of straightening crooked paths and smoothing out rough roads. With this in mind, ask everyone to take the felt-tip pens from underneath their seats and write or draw on their pebbles something in their lives that they think needs smoothing if Jesus is really to be Lord in their lives.

When everyone has finished, invite them to come to the front and silently place their pebbles in the manger. Explain that this is a sign that they recognise that the child of Christmas should be Lord of our lives, shaping them to be like his.

Fade out the wave soundtrack or music, then close with a short prayer that offers what has been written or drawn on the pebbles to God and ask for his Holy Spirit to work in our lives to shape us to be more like Jesus.

# For the gift of Jesus

*A prayer of thanks with actions for all ages*

**Leader:** For the great gift of Jesus born amongst us,
*(Arms stretched out to the side to indicate everyone)*
**All:** We thank you, Lord.
**Leader:** For the gift of Jesus more precious than gold,
*(Both hands cupped in front of you as if holding something very precious)*
**All:** We thank you, Lord.
**Leader:** For the gift of Jesus, Saviour of the world,
*(Make a large globe shape with both hands)*
**All:** We thank you, Lord.
**Leader:** For the gift of Jesus, our Lord and our King,
*(Both hands stretched up)*
**All:** We thank you, Lord.

# Accepting God's gift

*A simple prayer activity suitable for all ages together*

**You will need:** a Christmas tree, small gift tags for each member of the congregation (make these from last year's Christmas cards), pens or pencils

Distribute the gift tags and pens. Invite everyone to think about what they would like to say to God about his gift of new life through Jesus. They could: write a prayer; write 'Thank you' or their own name; *or* draw a smiling face, to indicate their acceptance of God's gift.

Invite people to come forward and hang their prayers on the Christmas tree.

# The Saviour is here!

*A meditation on the meaning of Jesus' presence with us*

**You will need:** *a display of the words of Isaiah 9:6,7*

Display the words of Isaiah 9:6,7. Before reading them aloud together, ask everyone to take particular note of each of the names that are given to Jesus, the God who came to earth.

Jesus is called Wonderful Advisor, Mighty God, Eternal Father and Prince of Peace.

Ask everyone to think about the difference it could make to them in the coming week if they were to remember that the person whom Isaiah describes in all these ways is with them.

Ask everyone to think quietly about what it means to have Jesus with us, for example:

Think about when you might need wise advice during the coming week. If you have difficult problems to solve at work, at school or at home, remember that the Wonderful Advisor is here!

If you are facing something that is very hard for you to do this week, remember that the Mighty God is here!

If you feel frightened or lonely, remember that the Eternal Father, who never stops caring for you, is here!

If you are in the middle of an argument or fight this week, remember that the Prince of Peace is here!

# Let light blaze

*Prayers for others suitable for all ages together*

Think of places around the world and locally where people are walking in darkness – full of fear, despair and anxiety. If you have a Christmas tree or advent candles, light them as each situation is mentioned; light a candle as a reminder of the Light of the World.

The world waited in darkness until the Light of the World came.
*Let light blaze everywhere!*
And now the good news of Jesus spreads throughout the world.
*Let light blaze everywhere!*
The Light brings blessings to women, men and children.
*Let light blaze everywhere!*
When the Light of the World shines on us, we know how to live.
*Let light blaze everywhere!*
Away with fear, despair and anxiety;
*Let light blaze everywhere!*
Let there be love, hope and peace in my heart and in yours.
*Let light blaze everywhere!*

# Following God's light

*A responsive prayer for Epiphany*

O God, giver of light to the world;
*Help us to follow your light.*
Like wise ones following a star;
*Help us to follow your light.*
When things go wrong;
*Help us to follow your light.*
When all is well;
*Help us to follow your light.*
Like travellers seeking your truth;
*Help us to follow your light.*

**Creative prayer**

## Salt dough decorations

*Easy Christmas tree decorations*

**You will need:** *salt dough, rolling pins, Christmas cutters, a large cloth, pencil, some ribbon to hang shapes*

Make some salt dough by mixing 300 g of plain flour and 300 g of salt with a tablespoon of oil and approximately 200 ml water.

Knead it on a floured surface until it is smooth and elastic. The dough can be stored in a plastic bag in the fridge.

Roll out the dough and cut out a Christmas shape. Make a hole in the top with a pencil. Bake the shapes in the oven for 10–20 minutes at Gas mark 4 or 180 °C.

## Handprint angels

*Simple enough for small children to make*

**You will need:** *trays of brightly coloured paint, A4 coloured sheets of card, glitter, string or ribbon, aprons, cover-up and clean-up equipment*

Give each child a sheet of card. Encourage them to do a handprint. Wash painty hands straight away.

Here comes the surprise! Add a circle at the top (a head) and some glitter, to make the handprint look like an angel!

When it is dry, cut the shape out and add a loop of ribbon or string to make a Christmas tree decoration.

## Make a manger

*A simple nativity scene for small children to make*

**You will need:** *egg carton lids or other boxes, sticky tape, wooden dolly pegs, tissue or scraps of fabric, hay or shredded paper, felt-tip pens*

Give each child a box to turn into a food box or 'manger' for animals. Fill this with hay or shredded paper.

Make a 'baby Jesus' figure from a wooden peg by drawing a face on the rounded end. Wrap the rest of the peg in tissue or fabric. Place the peg baby in the manger. (You could make a whole nativity scene with other peg dolls.)

As you make the manger, ask the children where they slept when they were babies. Why did they sleep in cots and prams? What did they have to keep them warm? Talk about how a hay box was a surprising place to put a baby – especially a baby as special as God's Son!

## Make a Christmas gift

*An easy gift for younger children to make*

**You will need:** *sheets of coloured tissue paper cut into 20 cm squares, wrapped sweets, small pictures and shapes cut from Christmas gift wrap, shiny ribbon, glue sticks*

Let each child choose three or four sheets of tissue in different colours and place them one on top of another on a table.

Give each one a few sweets to put in the centre.

Help them make a small bundle, gathering the edges of the paper together. Tie securely with the shiny ribbon (an adult may need to do this). Tease out the layers of tissue paper to make an attractive parcel. Let the children choose pieces of gift wrap to paste onto the parcel.

## 'Stained glass' Bible verse

*A decoration to display in a window*

**You will need:** *a gold or silver pen, A4 sheets of black paper, tissue paper, scissors, glue*

Use the gold or silver pen to write out the Bible verse on the black paper, except for the words 'light', 'shines' and 'world'. (The true *light* that *shines* on everyone was coming into the *world*.' John 1:9) In these places, cut out a star shape instead.

Cut out squares from the tissue paper to stick onto the back of the star shapes, making a stained glass effect. Write the words 'light', 'shines' and 'world' on the appropriate tissue star.

Display in a window so that the light shines through the stars.

## 'Jesus' banner

*A talking-point banner to make and display*

**You will need:** *big letters spelling 'J-e-s-u-s' cut from strong paper or card, collage and art materials (for example, tinsel, baubles, bells), a large piece of fabric (for example, a flat sheet), PVA glue, strong bamboo cane, a stapler*

This large-scale project can involve everyone. Ask volunteers to draw or paint a picture of Jesus as a baby while others decorate each letter in the name 'Jesus', using paint, collage or Christmas decorations. Explain to the non-readers what these letters spell.

Spread out the background fabric. Position the name letters and the pictures of Jesus. When you are all happy with the arrangement, glue the pieces into place. Make the fabric attractive with decorations, paper chains or strings of angels. Hang the banner on the bamboo, stapling it firmly into place.

## Advent wreath

*A decoration suitable for all ages to make*

**You will need:** *a ring of oasis (flower arranging base) plus a small piece of oasis to hold the central candle, four red candles and one white candle, evergreen foliage, red, white or purple flowers, rosettes of ribbon (wired), matches, a round tray and strong tape (this can be obtained at florists' shops)*

If using fresh greenery and flowers you will need to get a 'wet' oasis (pre-soaked in water). If using artificial greenery and flowers, the oasis needs to be 'dry'. Secure the oasis to the tray.

Let the children watch as you place four candles at equal distances around the ring of oasis, with the white one in the centre.

The children could help arrange the coniferous foliage at a lower level around the ring and put other evergreen foliage (for example, holly and variegated ivy) above it so that the ring is completely covered. (Be aware of health, safety and allergy issues.)

Add flowers and ribbon rosettes at regular intervals around the ring to provide colour.

Dim the light or shade the windows. Light the first candle and encourage the group to sit quietly as they watch the flame.

Say these words:

As the candle burns, it brings bright light to our room.
As the candle burns, the darkness disappears.
As we watch the candle flame flicker and burn,
We remember that God is here with us now.

## Make an angel

*A hanging angel for younger children to make*

**You will need:** *angel arms and face on page 78 copied onto white card, shiny decorations (sticky stars, gift ribbon, large sequins), a white disposable cup, washable PVA glue*

Prepare a cardboard angel face and pair of arms for each child.

Let the children cover the angel arms and cup with the shiny decorations.

Turn the cup upside down and assemble the angel by taping the arms to the back of the cup (angel body) and the face to the top at the front. Pierce a hole in the base of the cup and thread a length of gift ribbon through to make a hanging decoration.

## Surprise angel painting

*Wax-resistant painting for younger children*

**You will need:** *large sheets of white paper, white wax crayons or large white candles, powder paint mixed to a watery consistency or diluted ready-mixed paints, paint pots, a bold line drawing of an angel as on page 79*

Give each child a sheet of paper and a white wax crayon or candle. Help them to draw an angel on the paper. You may need to guide them through the process as the drawing will be hard to see.

Say that the children have made a surprise for each other. They can then paint all over the sheet of paper, one at a time to reveal the angels. Be surprised and excited each time!

For very small children, draw the angels before the session and tell them that you have made a surprise for them. Then simply allow the children to paint over the paper.

## The true light

*A candle Christmas card*

**You will need:** *copies of the candle card on page 81, scissors, colouring materials, glue, gold, orange, red or yellow paper, glitter*

Fold the paper from top to bottom, then in half sideways to make a card. Carefully cut out the panel on the front, including the layer beneath it, so that a pattern from the name 'Jesus' shows in the candle space. (Some adult help may be needed for this.) Let the children colour the cards, glue a paper flame at the top of the candle, and decorate with glitter.

# Mini screen

*Picture sequence to tell the Christmas story*

**You will need:** *a Bible, scissors, glue, colouring materials, an envelope, pictures from page 82, a strip of paper about 80 cm x 8 cm*

Colour the pictures and cut them out. Draw round one of them on the front of the envelope and cut out this panel.

Glue the pictures in order along the centre of the strip of paper, leaving about 5 cm at each end and between each one.

Cut down the sides of the envelope and then seal it as normal. Thread the strip of paper through the sides so that the pictures show one by one through the hole.

Read the story from the Bible (Luke 2:1–7), moving the strip to the next picture in sequence.

# Star decoration

*A tree decoration with a special meaning*

**You will need:** *an old CD for each child, coloured permanent pens, glitter and strong glue, string or yarn, 'star of David' template below..*

Show the template and explain that this shape is used as the symbol for King David. Jesus was part of David's family, just as God promised.

Give each child a CD and help them to position the template in the middle. Help them draw around the template in permanent pen. They can use the pens or glitter and glue to decorate the star shape.

Fix a loop of yarn or string on the back with sticky tape. Suggest the decoration is hung in a window or on a Christmas tree at home, to remind everyone of how God kept his promise.

# Lift-the-flap baby

*A 'thank you' card for small children to make*

**You will need:** *the picture , sheets of card in different sizes, sticky tape, crayons or felt-tip pens, glue sticks*

Glue the picture of Jesus in the centre of a sheet of card, leaving a broad border all around. Let the children decorate the border and colour the picture.

Write 'Thank you, God' on a sheet of card slightly larger than the Jesus picture.

Help the children line up the sheets of card, to cover the pictures of Jesus. Let the children choose which way they want the flaps to open; tape along the appropriate edge.

Hold the cards up and say: 'Thank you, God, for...' Lift the flap to reveal the surprise. This time, look at the pictures and say, 'Thank you, God, for baby Jesus.'

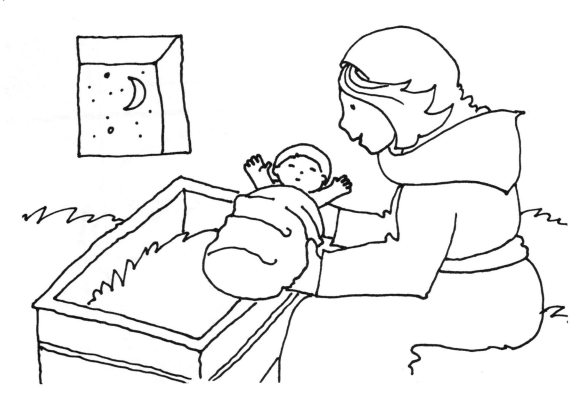

# Nativity figures

*Puppets or stand-up figures for younger children*

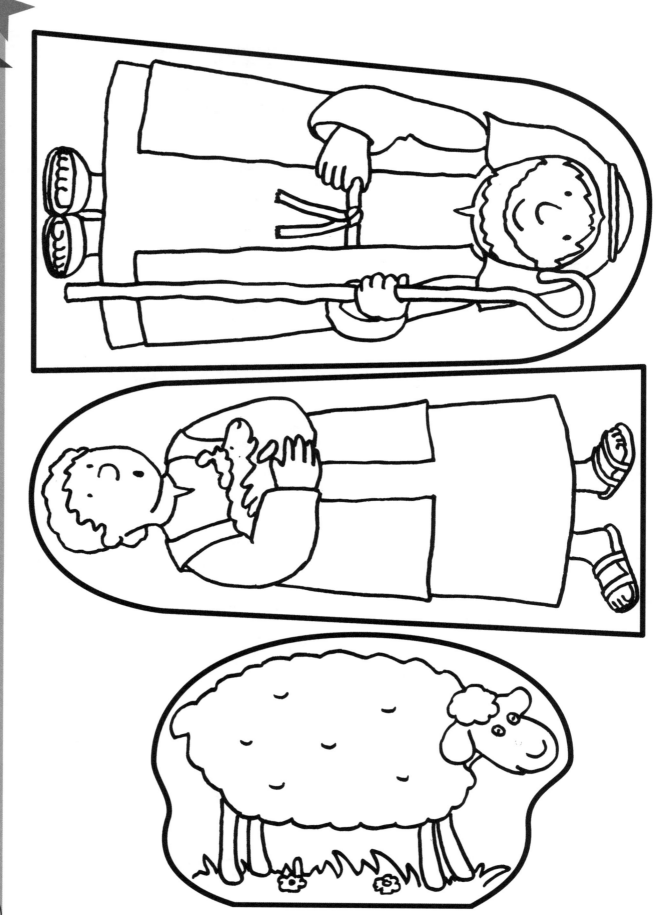

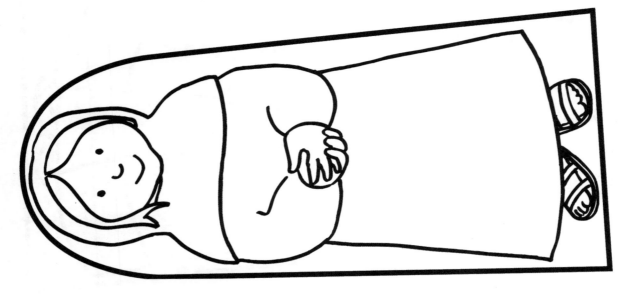

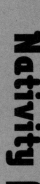

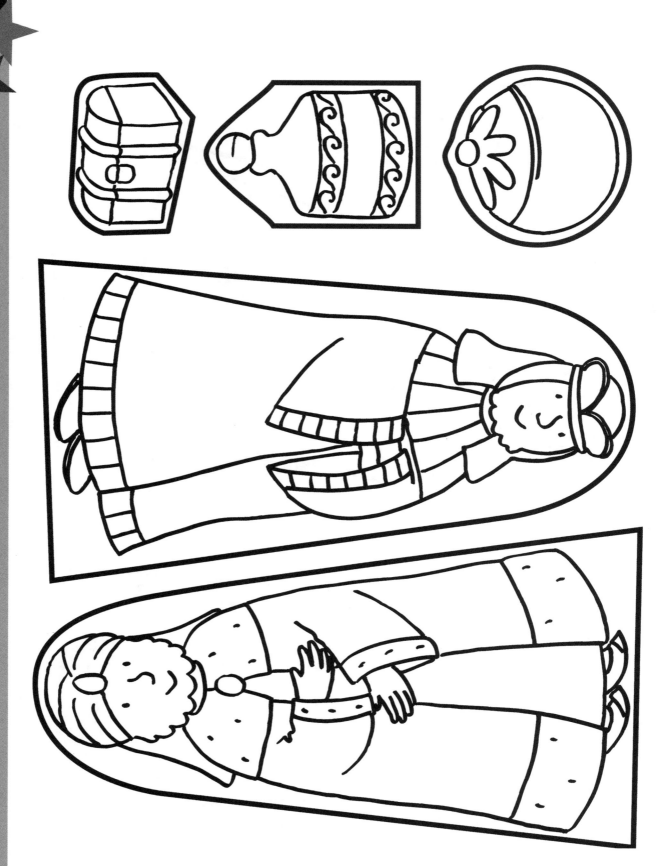

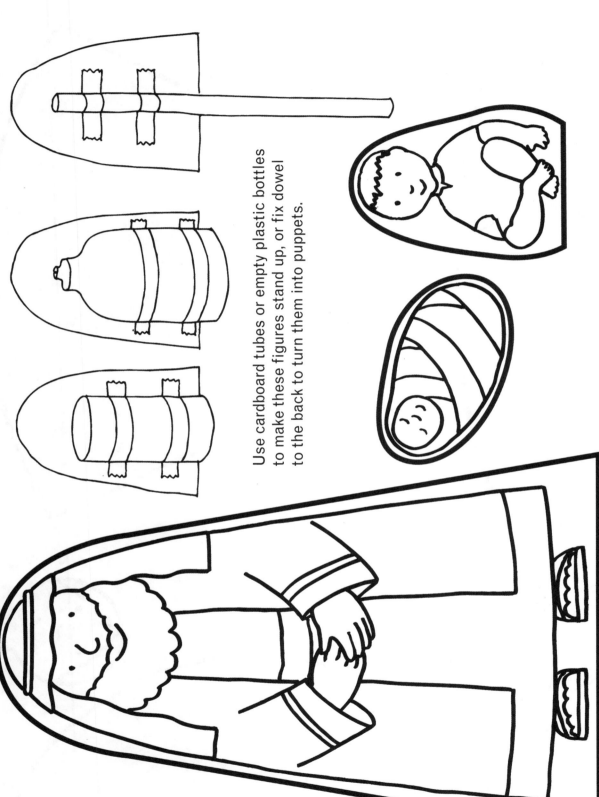

Use cardboard tubes or empty plastic bottles to make these figures stand up, or fix dowel to the back to turn them into puppets.

# Make an angel

# Angel templates

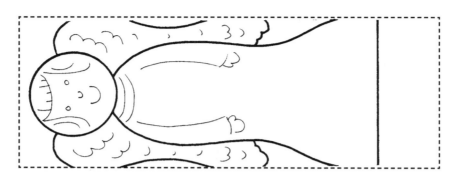

Template for concertina angels

Template for angel mobile

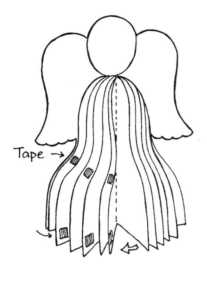

Tape →

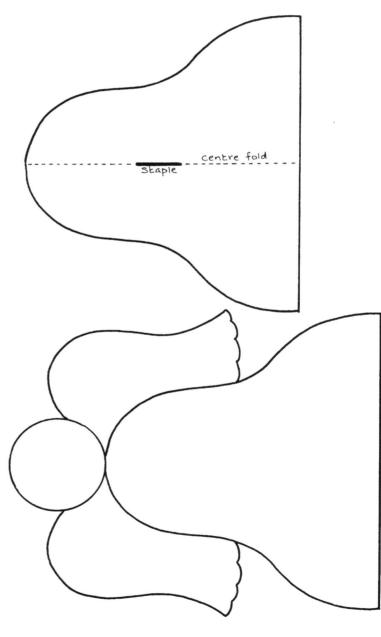

centre fold

staple

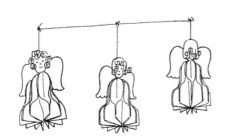

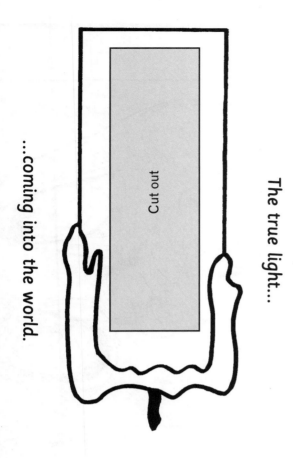

The true light...

...coming into the world.

Cut out

---

The true light that shines
on everyone was coming
into the world.

Cut out

John 1:9

---

# Happy Christmas!

JESUS is the light!

From:

# Mini screen

**Picture 1:** verses 1 and 2
**Picture 2:** verses 3 and 4
**Picture 3:** verse 5a
**Picture 4:** verses 5b–7a
**Picture 5:** verses 7b

Craft

80

Craft

81

# Christmas gift boxes

*For older children, young people or adults*

**You will need:** the box template copied onto card, glitter, coloured pens, sticky tape

Cut out the template – enough for each person. On the lid, write the words 'Remember the gift of God's Son' and then decorate the box with colours and glitter.

Make them into gift boxes, leaving the lid open.

A small gift can be placed inside.

# Shooting star

*A box model to tell the story of the wise men*

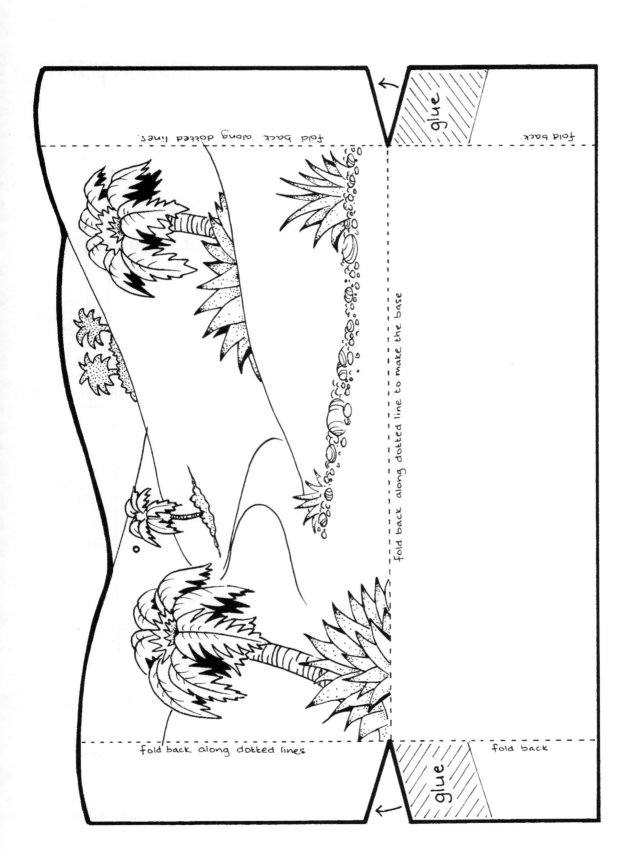

fold back along dotted lines.

fold back along dotted line to make the base

glue

fold back

fold back along dotted lines

glue

fold back

# Games

## Star hunt

*A simple game for small children*

**You will need:** *lots of silver cardboard stars of varying sizes (templates on page 83), glitter, tinsel, glue*

Hide the stars around the room. (Avoid high shelves or sharp corners.) Challenge the children to find as many of the stars as they can.

Play a game where you use the stars to make a trail around your room or building, for children and adults to follow together. (You could 'arrive' at your nativity scene.)

Sit down with all the stars in the centre of your circle. Ask the children which star they think the wise men might have followed and why. Which star would the children follow? What do the children know about the wise men? What kind of people were they? Why did God put the star in the sky?

## Night-time on the hillside

*A story game for younger children*

Tell the story of the shepherds from Luke 2:8–20.

Ask the children how they think the sleepy shepherds must have felt when all of a sudden an angel appeared in the night sky! Explain that we are going to act as the angels and the shepherds.

Teach them this rhyme:

Night-time on the hillside
Quiet with the sheep,
Angels wake the shepherds
From their restful sleep.
'Don't be afraid! I have good news.
Today, a Saviour was born for you.'

When they know it well, ask one child to lie down asleep pretending to be a shepherd and the rest of the children to walk in a circle around the 'shepherd', saying this rhyme.

When the children say, 'Don't be afraid!' the 'shepherd' jumps up and acts being afraid. If possible, give all the children a turn at being the 'shepherd'.

You can develop the game by dividing the children into three groups and label them 'angels', 'shepherds' and 'people'. The 'shepherds' and 'people' should pretend to be asleep. The 'angels' start the game by walking around the 'sleeping shepherds' saying the rhyme. The 'shepherds' should 'wake up' when the 'angels' say, 'Don't be afraid!'

Then invite the 'shepherds' to walk around the 'sleeping people'. Teach them this slightly different rhyme:

Night-time in the houses,
Dreaming of the sheep.
Shepherds wake the people,
From their restful sleep.

Then the 'people' 'wake up' when the 'shepherds' say, 'Don't be afraid!'

## Shepherd and angel game

*For younger children*

Divide the children into two groups: angels and shepherds. The 'shepherds' sit in the middle of the room in a circle. The 'angels' stand around the room.

The 'shepherds' close their eyes while the 'angels' creep up as quietly as possible behind them. When they are close to the 'shepherds', at your signal, they shout, 'Surprise! Jesus is born!'

The 'shepherds' then jump up and say, 'Let's go and see him!' They can run around the room or jump up and down on the spot, depending on the space available.

Change roles and play the game again.

## King Jesus

*A game for children who can read*

**You will need:** *a large picture of a manger (see page 88), sheets of card or paper, Blu-tack, blindfold (for volunteers only – shutting eyes is an alternative)*

Ask the children to tell you some words or phrases that describe Jesus the king, such as 'powerful' or 'glorious'. Write each one boldly on a small card or paper. Share these amongst the children.

Display the picture of the manger. Let the children take turns to be blindfolded and fix a label onto the picture, getting as near to where the baby would be without going on top of someone else's label.

Look at the picture together. Say that everyone had fun playing the game, but it also reminds us that the baby in the manger is the same person as King Jesus.

# Learn and remember

*A fun way of learning a Bible verse*

**You will need:** *the Bible verse (printed on paper), crackers*

Print the Bible verse below from the Good News Bible on slips of paper, one word on each slip, and push each one into a different cracker. Give everyone a cracker, pull them, and put the memory verse together. Explain that 'The Word' refers to God coming to earth as a human being.

'The Word became a human being and, full of grace and truth, lived among us.'
John 1:14a (GNB)

# Immanuel

*An active game for older children*

Say that one of the special names given to baby Jesus was 'Immanuel' which means 'God is with us'.

Show the children the following words and accompanying actions:

'Home' *(Children run to one end of the room.)*
'School' *(Children run to the other end of the room.)*
'Friends' *(Wave.)*
'Family' *(Wrap arms around yourself.)*
'Happy' *(Thumbs up.)*
'Sad' *(Thumbs down.)*
'Sick' *(Clutch stomach.)*
'Lonely' *(Shake head and look sad.)*
'Playing' *(Run on the spot.)*
'All the time' *(Make a circle in the air with your arms.)*

Do the actions and each time you say the word, preface it with: 'God is with us when we are…'
For example: if you say, 'God is with us when we are at *home*', the children would run to the appropriate end of the room.

This could be played as an elimination game, or with different children calling.

# Christmas card hunt

*A game to discover the true meaning of Christmas*

**You will need:** *a variety of Christmas pictures or words, including one with Jesus on*

Find some pictures – the front of old Christmas cards or magazine pictures – that show Christmassy items (for example, tinsel, snowmen, Christmas trees). You will also need just one picture, smaller than the rest, of Jesus as a baby.

In advance, hide the cards around the room. Give everyone one minute to find a card that portrays the true meaning of Christmas. At the end of the game, take a look at the cards. All show things to do with Christmas, but only one portrays the true meaning of Christmas – the one with Jesus. Point out that the card with Jesus is smaller than the rest, and was therefore harder to find. It may be hard to find the true meaning of Christmas amidst the presents, tinsel and lights.

# Christmas wrapping

*A game for older children*

**You will need:** *cheap Christmas wrapping paper, sticky tape, blindfolds, recycling bags*

Take about five volunteers out of the room and blindfold them.

Wrap five more volunteers in Christmas wrapping. Wrappers should do everything they can to conceal anything that would identify the person under the wrapping: for example wrappers should make sure the person's shoes are covered. Wrappers may also add cushions to make the person appear bigger, or taller than they really are.

The five blindfolded volunteers are brought back into the room and each takes off his or her blindfold.

They are each given a volunteer, and must guess who it is. (Make sure you recycle all your used wrapping paper!)

After the game, explain that God gave his Son to us at Christmas, and his packaging was so unexpected, that many people did not recognize the world's best Christmas present for what and who he was.

Another way this idea could be presented is to wrap up obvious-shaped objects in an unusual manner.

# Chocolate shepherd!

*A game for older children*

**You will need:** *a large bar of chocolate, a large plate, knives and forks, a cloak, a tea towel for each child, a pair of gloves, dice*

The children sit in a circle with the props in the centre. Each child has their own tea towel and should practise putting it on their head to look like a shepherd. The children take it in turns to throw the dice.

When someone throws a six, he puts on the cloak, gloves and his own tea towel. He should try and eat the chocolate bar with the knife and fork, while the dice is still going round the circle.

As soon as someone else throws a six, the person in the middle must take off the dressing-up clothes and the next person dresses up. An adult should collect the used cutlery and hand out clean cutlery to the new player. Some players will get the chance to eat a lot of chocolate; others will not even have the time to get started!

# Pin the tail!

*A game for all children and young people*

**You will need:** a simple nativity scene (from a book or drawn yourself), paper, pens, Blu-tack, blindfold

Before you play the game, alter the picture so that you remove some of the details. For example, you might remove a lamb, a star and an angel – it all depends on what the details in the picture you have chosen. Removing details from pictures is easily done with correction fluid or on a computer picture editing programme. Reproduce the items you removed on paper (either by drawing the items or making another copy of the picture) and cut them out. Stick a blob of Blu-tack on the back of each one.

Blindfold a volunteer and give them the pieces you have cut out. Challenge them to stick each piece on in the original place on the picture. Record how close they are to being correct and play again with another volunteer.

This is harder than 'pin the tail on the donkey', as the players don't know which bit they are sticking where! It also means you can have more than one winner.

## True or false quiz

Choose from the following questions:

Many prophets long ago told of Jesus' birth. (True)

Mary and Joseph lived in Bethlehem. (False)

Mary and Joseph didn't know that their baby was going to be special. (False)

Mary and Joseph were married when Jesus was born. (False)

Jesus was born in a palace. (False)

It was snowing when Jesus was born. (False)

Jesus' bed was a cattle trough. (True)

Everyone in the world knew that God's special baby had been born. (False)

Mary's son's name would be Jesus which means 'Holy One'. (False)

The name Jesus means 'God will save his people from their sins'. (True)

An angel spoke to Mary about having a son. (True)

Mary was told she'd find Jesus under an apple tree. (False)

The son would be a long-distance relative of King David (the one who killed Goliath). (True)

Mary didn't believe God would use her in such a way. (False)

God picked Mary because she wanted to be rich and famous. (False)

Mary would become pregnant by the power of the Holy Spirit. (True)

Jesus was both God and human. (True)

Jesus was actually Joseph's son, and turned into God later. (False)

Jesus would be king of a kingdom for the whole of his life. (True)

There were three wise men. (False or questionable!)

The wise men followed a star. (True)

According to the Bible the names of the wise men were Casper, Melchior and Balthazar. (False)

There was no room for Mary and Joseph at the inn. (True)

Jesus was laid to sleep in the hay. (True)

An ox and donkey watched the Baby Jesus. (False)

## Story quiz

**You will need:** *a sheet of paper and a pen for each team or person*

Explain that as you tell the story, there will be questions with four possible answers. Each person should decide if they think the answer is 'a', 'b', 'c' or 'd' and write down the appropriate letter.

Read the following story:

When it was nearly time for Jesus to be born, someone called for a census to count the people. Was it a) King Herod, b) Emperor Augustus, c) Governor Quirinius, d) Pontius Pilate? He wanted everyone to be counted, and so he ordered that a) everyone had to travel to Rome, b) everyone had to go to the local synagogue, c) everyone had to be at home on a certain day, d) everyone had to go to their home town.

So Mary and Joseph had to leave the place where they were living and go to a) Bethlehem, b) Jerusalem, c) Nazareth, d) Jericho. Joseph had to go there because he was from the family of a) King Saul, b) King David, c) Samson, d) Daniel. Bethlehem was known as 'the town of David'.

Mary was engaged to Joseph and travelled with him to Bethlehem. When they arrived, they had trouble finding a room to spend the night. This was because a) they didn't have enough money to pay, b) they arrived after dark, c) they were dirty and smelly after travelling so far, d) everywhere was already full of other guests.

Jesus was born in a stable and Mary wrapped him up to keep him warm and cosy. Then Jesus slept a) in Mary's arms, b) in Joseph's arms, c) on prickly hay, d) on clean bedding.

The correct answers in the given sequence are: b) Emperor Augustus, d) everyone had to go to their home town, a) Bethlehem, b) King David, d) everywhere was already full of other guests, c) on prickly hay.

# Christmas wordsearch 1

*Find the following words in our Christmas wordsearch*

| | | | |
|---|---|---|---|
| TRUSTED | TOGETHER | DREAM | BABY |
| JOSEPH | LISTENED | ANGEL | PROPHECY |
| MARY | OBEYED | MARRIED | |

| | | | | | | | | |
|---|---|---|---|---|---|---|---|---|
| T | R | U | S | T | E | D | I | M |
| D | E | N | E | T | S | I | L | P |
| M | A | N | M | O | U | E | L | R |
| G | O | H | A | G | M | D | I | O |
| S | L | P | R | E | A | W | B | P |
| Y | E | E | R | T | R | E | I | H |
| B | G | S | I | H | Y | T | H | E |
| A | N | O | E | E | U | S | W | C |
| B | A | J | D | R | E | A | M | Y |

# Christmas wordsearch 2

*A more complicated wordsearch!*

ANNA ELIZABETH JESUS QUIRINIUS
ANGEL FIRSTBORN JOHN SHEPHERD
BABY GABRIEL JOSEPH SIMEON
BETHLEHEM HEROD MARY STAR
CENSUS INN MICAH WISE MEN
DREAM ISAIAH NAZARETH ZECHARIAH

| Z | E | C | H | A | R | I | A | H | F | E | R | Y | B |
| W | L | G | E | N | H | W | S | I | S | A | I | A | E |
| I | I | A | R | N | D | W | I | S | S | F | O | R | T |
| S | Z | B | O | A | S | J | E | S | U | A | N | G | H |
| F | A | R | D | M | I | U | D | L | E | C | I | E | L |
| I | B | I | N | I | M | O | S | H | A | M | B | A | E |
| R | E | E | N | C | E | N | H | J | O | S | E | P | H |
| S | T | L | T | A | O | A | E | Z | A | B | T | N | E |
| T | H | J | O | H | N | Z | P | E | D | R | E | A | M |
| B | Y | K | M | E | R | G | H | C | J | O | H | M | R |
| O | A | N | A | Z | A | R | E | T | H | E | I | N | M |
| R | N | B | R | A | E | B | R | L | F | I | S | T | B |
| N | N | E | Y | B | A | C | D | I | R | N | Q | U | E |
| Q | R | G | M | A | Q | U | I | R | I | N | I | U | S |

# Bauble hunt

*A fun quiz for Christmas*

For this quiz, you will need baubles of different colours. These are available quite cheaply from many DIY stores, department stores and other shops. You may already have enough yourself!

## Preparation

Gather together about twenty baubles per team – try to have a different colour for each team. Before the quiz, hide ten baubles of each colour around the room.

## How to play

Split your group into teams and tell everyone which colour their team is looking for. When you give the signal, everyone searches for the baubles of their colour. When they find one, they should bring it to you. The first team to bring a bauble to you is asked a question. If they get the question right, they keep the bauble. If they get the question wrong, or don't know the answer, offer the question to the other team(s). If another team gets it right, they get a bauble of their own colour, from the ten you still have. At the end of the quiz, the team with the most baubles is the winner!

## Questions

Use these questions or write some of your own. You may find it helpful to read out the more unusual passages of the Christmas story before you start (for example, Zechariah and Elizabeth or Simeon and Anna).

1 Who was the son of Zechariah and Elizabeth?
*John*
2 Where was Zechariah when he saw the angel?
*In the temple*
3 What happened to Zechariah when he didn't believe what the angel told him?
*He wasn't able to speak until his son was born.*
4 Who was Mary engaged to be married to?
*Joseph*
5 What was the name of the angel who visited Mary?
*Gabriel*
6 What did the angel say was impossible to God?
*Nothing!*
7 Who did Mary visit when she was pregnant?
*Elizabeth*
8 What was Joseph planning to do when he found out Mary was pregnant?
*Quietly call off the marriage.*
9 What happened to change his mind?
*He was visited by an angel in a dream.*

10 Who was Emperor at the time of Jesus' birth?
*Augustus*
11 What did Augustus order everyone in the empire to do?
*To have their names listed in record books so they could pay taxes.*
10 Where did Joseph and Mary have to go?
*Bethlehem*
11 Why was Jesus put on a bed of hay?
*Because there was no room for them at the inn.*
12 Who were in the fields above Bethlehem?
*Shepherds*
13 Who visited the shepherds in the fields?
*An angel*
14 What did the angel say to the shepherds?
*Don't be afraid! I have good news for you. A Saviour has been born for you in King David's home town (Bethlehem). You will know who he is because he is dressed in baby clothes and lying on a bed of hay.*
15 What were all the angels doing?
*Praising God in heaven!*
16 What did the shepherds do next?
*They went to visit the baby lying on the hay.*
17 Where did Mary and Joseph take Jesus to when he was eight days old?
*The temple in Jerusalem, where he was named Jesus.*
18 Who did Mary and Joseph meet in the temple?
*Simeon*
19 What did Simeon do with the baby Jesus?
*He took him in his arms and praised and thanked God for him.*
20 Someone else was also in the temple, who was she?
*Anna, a prophet.*
21 How old was Anna?
*Eighty-four years old.*
22 Who was king at the time of Jesus' birth?
*Herod*
23 Who followed a star to find Jesus?
*Wise men*
24 How many wise men were there?
*The Bible doesn't say.*
25 Who were the wise men looking for?
*Jesus*
26 What did the wise men want to do when they found Jesus?
*Worship him.*
27 What gifts did they give to Mary for Jesus?
*Myrrh, frankincense and gold.*
28 Did the wise men go and tell Herod where Jesus was?
*No, they went a different way.*

Code No 17450/23

| THE PROPHECY X-FILE | ASSIGNMENT TWO: |
|---|---|

The following references relate to someone important. They have been intercepted at great cost. We need to discover whether this person is here. Read each of these references below and then check them off as you read the events recorded in Luke 2:1–7.

Genesis 3:15 ................ ☐          Isaiah 11:2 ................... ☐

Genesis 17:19 .............. ☐          Isaiah 50:6 ................... ☐

Genesis 18:18 .............. ☐          Isaiah 53:3 ................... ☐

Deuteronomy 18:15 ......... ☐          Isaiah 53:7 ................... ☐

Psalm 16:10 ................ ☐          Isaiah 53:12 .................. ☐

Psalm 22:6–8 ............... ☐          Jeremiah 31:15 ............... ☐

Psalm 22:16 ................ ☐          Daniel 9:25 .................. ☐

Psalm 22:18 ................ ☐          Hosea 11:1 ................... ☐

Psalm 110:4 and                          Micah 5:2 .................... ☐

Hebrews 6:20; .............. ☐          Zechariah 9:9 ................ ☐

Isaiah 7:14 ................ ☐          Zechariah 11:12 .............. ☐

Isaiah 9:1,2 ............... ☐          Zechariah 12:10 ............. ☐

Isaiah 9:7 ................. ☐

**IF THESE BOXES ARE NOT CHECKED WE WILL HAVE TO LEAVE THIS X-FILE OPEN. IT WILL REQUIRE FURTHER INVESTIGATION.**

# Christmas cookery

## Baby in manger biscuits

**You will need:** *jelly babies, rich tea fingers, ready-to-roll icing, small pastry cutters, cocktail sticks (optional)*

Give each person a small piece of icing to flatten and cut out a circle.

Wrap the jelly baby in the circle so that the face is still showing and the icing forms a blanket around it.

Make a pillow from the rest of the piece of icing.

Lay the baby on the biscuit with its head on the pillow.

You can use a cocktail stick to score a pattern on to the blanket, if you wish.

## Shortbread stars

**You will need:** *a wooden spoon, a rolling pin, cutting 'star' shape, a baking sheet, a wire rack, ingredients (125 g butter, 55 g caster sugar, 180 g plain flour)*

Heat the oven to 190 °C (375 °F, Gas mark 5).

Beat the butter and the sugar together until it is pale in colour.

Stir in the flour to get a smooth paste. Turn onto a clean work surface and gently roll out until the paste is 1 cm thick.

Cut into stars and sprinkle with a little extra caster sugar. Place on a baking sheet and chill for 20 minutes. Bake in the oven for 15–20 minutes until lightly golden. Cool on a wire rack.

## Fondant stars

**You will need:** *a small tin of condensed milk, 1 kg icing sugar, glacé lemon slices, lemon juice, yellow food colouring, a wooden spoon, a rolling pin, knife or 'star' cutter*

Empty the condensed milk into a large bowl. Slowly mix in the icing sugar to make a thick paste. (Use a wooden spoon.)

Add a few drops of lemon juice and yellow food colouring and work these into the paste, too.

Dust the surface with icing sugar and roll out the paste using a dusted rolling pin.

Cut into star shapes using a knife or star cutter and decorate them with the lemon pieces.

Allow them to dry for about 30 minutes.

## Angel cakes

**You will need:** *cake cases, ingredients for 24 cakes: 100 g margarine or butter, 100 g sugar, 100 g self-raising flour, 2 eggs, whipped cream or butter cream, jam, icing sugar*

Cream together the sugar and margarine.

Beat in the eggs and then stir in the flour.

Spoon the mixture into the cake cases. Bake for 10–15 minutes at 375 °F (190 °C, Gas mark 5).

Leave to cool and then cut a circle out of the top of each. Fill the top with jam and a little whipped or butter cream.

Cut the top slice of each in half and place them in the cream to look like wings. Dust all the cakes with icing sugar.

## Marshmallow popcorn tree

**You will need:** *a big bowl, waxed paper, a saucepan, 250 g ready-to-eat popcorn, 60 g margarine, 200 g marshmallows, half a pack of lime-flavoured jelly, green food colouring, small sweets to decorate the tree*

Place the popcorn in a big bowl and place a sheet of waxed paper or baking parchment on a flat surface.

Melt the margarine and marshmallows in a non-stick saucepan, and then stir in the jelly cubes until melted. Add the green colouring.

Pour this over the popcorn in the bowl and stir to coat it very quickly. Tip all of it onto the paper and with dampened hands mould it into a Christmas tree shape. Decorate it with sweets.

After it has set, the tree can be cut into chunks with a sharp knife.

Be aware of food allergies. Check that all the children are safe to handle and can eat the ingredients. Also be alert to hygiene, health and safety issues.

# Songs and rhymes for younger children

## Baby Jesus

*A song to the tune of 'Baa, baa, black sheep'*

Baby Jesus, *(Rock arms.)*
You're the special one. *(Cross arms over chest.)*
We will worship *(Hold out arms with palms up.)*
God's own Son. *(Point up.)*
Sweet little baby, you're lying so still, *(Rock arms.)*
We will love and worship you; yes, yes, we will!
*(Cross arms over chest and nod your head.)*

## Sing good news

*A song to the tune of 'Jingle bells'*

Sing good news, sing good news, sing a happy song.
When we have good news to tell, we sing it loud and long.
Sing good news, sing good news, happy news we bring,
Let's do what the angels do; let's sing, sing, sing, sing, sing!

'Off you go,' the angel said, 'off to Bethlehem.
Go and look until you find, a newborn baby king.'
Sing good news, sing good news, happy news we bring,
Let's do what the angels do; let's sing, sing, sing, sing, sing!

Here we go; here we go, off to Bethlehem!
We have looked and we have found, Jesus the baby king.
Sing good news, sing good news, sing a happy song.
When we have good news to tell, we sing it loud and long.

## Here are the sheep

*An action rhyme*

Here are the sheep, asleep on the hill,
*(Left hand raised, fingers curled in.)*
Here are the shepherds, watching them still.
*(Wiggle the two longest fingers of right hand.)*
Bright shining angels came to send the good news.
*(Wiggle all your fingertips quickly in the air.)*
A baby is born for me and for you.
*(Rock a baby; point to yourself and others.)*
Dear God, now it's Christmas, with presents and fun,
*(Hands together; then spin hands in a circle.)*
We thank you for your gift of your own precious Son.
*(Extend hands; rock a baby.)*

## Shepherds

*An action rhyme*

This rhyme, with mimed actions, can be used to introduce or revise the telling of the Christmas story.

An adult can act the part of the angel, with everyone else acting as shepherds. Or divide the group so half the children are angels and half are shepherds.

Shepherds sat and watched their sheep,
*(Sit or crouch down.)*
One dark and starry night.
Shepherds saw an angel,
*(Cover eyes.)*
And a bright, bright light.
'Get up! Get up!' the angel said.
*(Stand up.)*
'Listen to what I say:
Mary had a baby boy
In Bethlehem today.'
Shepherds hurried off to see,
*(Run on the spot.)*
And through the stable door,
*(Mime opening door.)*
They saw the baby Jesus
In a manger full of straw.
Happy, happy shepherds,
*(Clap twice.)*
To be the first to hear
Of Mary and her baby boy.
*(Rock arms.)*
In a stable near.

## Dark, dark, dark

Dark, dark, dark, it's dark on the hillside.
Dark, dark, dark, alone with the sheep.
Dark, dark, dark, no stars and no sunshine.
Dark, dark, dark, I just want to sleep.

Light, light, light, a light in the night-time.
Light, light, light, in the sky up above.
Light, light, light, a beautiful angel!
Light, light, light, he tells of God's love.

'News, news, news, good news,' says the angel.
News, news, news, for everyone.
News, news, news, to make the people happy.
News, news, news, your Saviour has come.

Praise, praise, praise, with angels on the hillside.
Praise, praise, praise, our God who loves us so.
Praise, praise, praise, for the birth of the baby.
Praise, praise, praise, as to Bethlehem we go.

Look, look, look at the baby as he lies there.
Look, look, look, he is Christ the Lord.
Look, look, look, tell all that God has told us.
Look, look, look, he's worshipped and adored.

Run, run, run, through the streets, back to the hillside.
Run, run, run, give the news to everyone.
Run, run, run, shout to God and sing his praises.
Run, run, run, this baby is God's Son!

## Shining star

*Refrain:*

*Shining star, shining star,*
*Shining very bright.*
*Shining star, shining star,*
*Lighting up the night.*

Guide us where the Saviour's lying,
Can we see his little bed?
Can we kneel and bring our treasures,
Worship at his head?

*Refrain:*
*Shining star, shining star,*
*Shining very bright.*
*Shining star, shining star,*
*Lighting up the night.*

Guide us where the Saviour's lying,
We can see his little bed.
We can kneel and bring our treasures,
Worship at his head.

*Refrain:*
*Shining star, shining star,*
*Shining very bright.*
*Shining star, shining star,*
*Lighting up the night.*

## Zechariah's song

God is good! His plan is working!
Promises to send a Saviour,
Promises to show his kindness,
Coming true before our eyes!

God is good! His plan is working!
My son, John, will show the way.
Promises to get us ready,
Coming true before our eyes!

God is good! His plan is working!
We will learn to say we're sorry;
Promises to forgive us,
Coming true before our eyes!

God is good! His plan is working!
Jesus' light will shine on all;
Promises of peace and mercy,
Coming true before our eyes!

## This very day

*A song to the tune 'When the saints go marching in':*
This very day, this very day,
This very day in Bethlehem
Was born a baby, your Saviour;
He is Jesus Christ the Lord.

## The journey of adventure

*See page 96 for sheet music.*

It was a journey of adventure,
Following a star.
But God was there to guide them,
Those wise men from afar.

Sometimes there is sadness,
And we sometimes cry,
But when we follow Jesus,
He's always close near by.

So will you follow Jesus,
Wherever you are from?
Join in God's adventure;
He'll guide you all life long.

© Lorna Sabbagh, 2004

If using the song with children, on the following words of the song try out these actions:

**journey** – jump forward with feet together;
**adventure** – raise both arms straight in the air and lower them again;
**following** – jump with feet together and turn one-quarter clockwise. Repeat until you are facing in the opposite direction.

These actions are on the first beat of every bar.

## Celebrate!

Come on and celebrate!
Gone is the night
The people who walked in darkness
Have seen a great light.

Come on and celebrate!
Darkness disappears
In the highest heavens
Angel hosts appear.

Come on and celebrate!
Shepherds and shepherd-boys
The hearts that once feared
Are now filled with joy.

Come on and celebrate!
Night turns to morn
In the city of King David
A child is born.

Come on and celebrate!
The Word is made flesh
In a manger so lowly
Lies Immanuel.

©Tanya Ferdinandusz

## Our Christmas story

A woman gives birth,
Our God descends to earth.
A star is born,
Our night turns to dawn.
Angels proclaim,
Our lips acclaim.
Shepherds adore,
Our eyes glow.
Wise men bow low,
Our hearts overflow.
This is our Christmas story;
To God be the glory.

©Tanya Ferdinandusz

## Your Christmas

*A poem to use as a discussion starter about the true meaning of Christmas*

The meaning of Christmas is all very clear.
It's turkey and tinsel and parties and beer.
It's rowing with aunties and sisters and Dad
And saying the pudding has made you feel bad.
It's looking at presents you never will wear,
And moaning how life is – well, not very fair;
Coz your cousin's got lots of things you never had
And your mum is now yelling at Granny and Dad.
Your brother is crying coz the battery is flat
And he can't use his toy and he's kicking the cat!
Yes, the telly is boring, the turkey is tough.
Christmas? Huh! Christmas! Have you had enough?!

# The journey of adventure

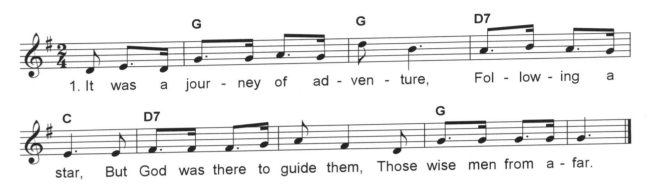

1. It was a jour - ney of ad - ven - ture, Fol - low - ing a

star, But God was there to guide them, Those wise men from a - far.

2. Sometimes there is sadness,
   And we sometimes cry,
   But when we follow Jesus
   He's always close near by.

3. So will you follow Jesus,
   Wherever you are from?
   Join in God's adventure,
   He'll guide you all life long.

© Lorna Sabbagh 2004